The Boat Who Wouldn't Float

The Boat Who

Wouldn't Float

Farley Mowat

Illustrated by Marc G. P. Berthier

McClelland and Stewart Limited

Hardbound edition: 0-7710-6586-8
Trade paperback edition: 0-7710-6587-6

The Canadian Publishers
McClelland and Stewart Limited
25 Hollinger Road, Toronto

Printed and bound in Canada

**For her friends who have
loved her despite her faults:
to Claire, Jack, Théo,
Peter, Albert, Andy, Angus,
Sandy, David, Peggy, John,
Dale, Don, and all the others —
but in particular to Mike
Donovan who will voyage no more
upon the unquiet waters.**

Books by Farley Mowat

People of the Deer (1952)
The Regiment (1955, new edition 1973)
Lost in the Barrens (1956)
The Dog Who Wouldn't Be (1957)
The Grey Seas Under (1959)
The Desperate People (1959)
Owls in the Family (1961)
The Serpent's Coil (1961)
The Black Joke (1962)
Never Cry Wolf (1963, new edition 1973)
Westviking (1965)
The Curse of the Viking Grave (1966)
Canada North (1967)
This Rock Within the Sea (with John de Visser) (1968)
The Boat Who Wouldn't Float (1969, new edition 1974)
Sibir (1970, new edition 1973)
A Whale for the Killing (1972)
Wake of the Great Sealers (with David Blackwood) (1973)

Edited by Farley Mowat

Coppermine Journey (1958)
The Top of the World trilogy
   Ordeal by Ice (1960, revised edition 1973)
   The Polar Passion (1967, revised edition 1973)
   Tundra (1973)

Contents

1 *Conception*

I HAVE an ingrained fear of auctions dating back to the third year of my life. In that year my father attended an auction as a means of passing an aimless afternoon, and he came away from it the bewildered possessor of thirty hives of bees and all the paraphernalia of an apiarist. Unable to rid himself of his purchase he became, perforce, a beekeeper, and for the next two years I lived almost exclusively on a diet of soda biscuits and honey. Then the gods smiled on us and all the bees died of something called foul brood, enabling us to return to some semblance of a normal life.

Auctions remain associated in my subconscious mind with great catastrophes. I normally avoid them like the plague, but one April day not many years ago I too fell victim to the siren call. It happened in a sleepy little Lake Ontario

town which once had been a major port for the great fleets of barley schooners that vanished forever shortly after the turn of the century. In that town there lived a ship-chandler who refused to accept the coming of steam and the death of sail, and who kept his shop and stock intact for half a century waiting for the day when a sailorman would again come knocking on his door. None did. He died, and his heirs decided to auction off the old man's junk so they could turn the building into a pool hall.

I happened to be passing through that town on auction day accompanied by a young lady for whom I had conceived a certain passion. However *her* passion was primarily reserved for auctions. When she saw the auction sign she insisted that we attend. I steeled myself to buy nothing but as I stood in the dim and ancient store which was still redolent of stockholm tar, oilskins, and dusty canvas, something snapped within me.

Amongst the attitudes I acquired from my father was a romantic and Conradian predilection for the sea and ships. Like him I had often found surcease from the miseries I brought upon myself by spending hours immersed in books about the cruises of small boats to far-distant corners of the oceanic world. Ten years before the day of the auction I had anchored myself to a patch of eroded sand-hills in central Ontario about as far from the sea as a man could get. There I had laboured to make grass, trees, vegetables, and mine own self take root. My labours had been in vain. Drought killed the grass. Sawflies and rabbits girdled the trees. Wireworms ate the vegetables. Far from rooting me into the Good Earth, a decade of servitude to the mingy soil only served to fuel a spirit of rebellion the intensity of which I had not begun to suspect until I stood in the old ship-chandler's store physically surrounded by a world I had only previously known in the imagination.

I bought. I bought, and I bought, and I bought. I bought enough nautical gear out of another age to fill an outbuilding on my parched little farm. I am my father's son; and so the story of the bees had to repeat itself to an inevitable conclusion.

It happens that I have a friend who is a publisher and who feels much the same way about the book business as I do about dirt farming. Jack McClelland is a romantic although he blanches at the word and vehemently denies it. During the war he served as skipper of M.T.B.'s (Motor Torpedo Boats) and other such small and dashing craft and although he returned at war's end to the drabness of the business world, his spirit remained on the bridge of an M.T.B. streaking through the grey Atlantic wastes, guns blazing at the dim spectres of German E-boats hopelessly trying to evade their fates. Jack owns a cottage on the Muskoka Lakes and there he keeps an old-fashioned, knife-bowed, mahogany launch which in the dark of the moon sometimes metamorphoses into an M.T.B. to the distress of occasional lovers drifting on the still waters in canoes.

One night a few weeks after I bought the departed chandler's stock, Jack McClelland and I were moored to a bar in Toronto. It was a dismal day in a dismal city so we stayed moored to the bar for several hours. I kept no notes of what was said nor do I recall with clarity how it all came to pass. I know only that before the night ended we were committed to buying ourselves an ocean-going vessel in which to roam the salt seas over.

We decided we should do things the old-fashioned way (we both have something of the Drake and Nelson complex) and this meant buying an old-fashioned boat; the kind of wooden boat that once was sailed by iron men.

The only place we knew where such a boat might be procured was in the remote and foggy island of Newfoundland. Consequently one morning in early May I flew off to that island's ancient capital, St. John's, where I had arranged to meet a red-bearded, coldly blue-eyed iconoclast named Harold Horwood who was reputed to know more about Newfoundland's scattered little outport villages than any living man. Despite the fact that I was a mainlander, and Harold

4

abhors mainlanders, he had agreed to help me in my quest. I am not sure why he did so but perhaps the unravelling of this chronicle will provide a hint.

Harold took me to visit scores of tiny fishing villages clinging like cold treacle to the wave-battered cliffs of the great island. He showed me boats ranging from fourteen-foot dories to the rotting majesty of a five-hundred-ton, three-masted schooner. Unfortunately, those vessels that were still sufficiently seaworthy to leave the wharf were not for sale, and those that could be had within my range (Jack had astutely placed a limit of a thousand dollars on the purchase price) were either so old and tired that piss-a-beds (the local name for dandelions) were sprouting from their decks, or they were taking a well-earned rest on the harbour bottom with only their upperworks awash.

Time was drawing on and we were no forwarder. Harold's red beard jutted at an increasingly belligerent angle; his frosty eyes took on a gimlet stare and his temper grew worse and worse. He was not used to being thwarted and he did not like it. He arranged to have a news item printed in the papers describing the arrival of a rich mainlander who was looking for a local schooner.

Two days later he informed me that he had found the perfect vessel. She was, he said, a small two-masted schooner of the type known generally as a jack-boat and, more specifically, as a Southern Shore bummer. I can't say that the name enthralled me, but by this time I, too, was growing desperate so I agreed to go and look at her.

She lay hauled out at Muddy Hole, a small fishing village on the east coast of the Avalon Peninsula—a coast that is rather inexplicably called the Southern Shore, perhaps because it lies south of St. John's and St. John's is, in its own eyes at least, the centre of the universe.

Tourist maps showed Muddy Hole as being connected to St. John's by road. This was a typical Newfoundland "jolly." Muddy Hole was not connected to St. John's at all except by a tenuous trail which, it is believed, was made some centuries ago by a very old caribou who was not only blind but also afflicted with the staggers.

In any event it took us six hours to follow where he had led. It was a typical spring day on the east coast of the island. A full gale was blowing from seaward, hurling slanting rain heavily against the car. The Grand Banks fog, which is forever lurking just off the coast, had driven in over the high headlands obscuring everything from view. Guided by some aboriginal instinct inherited from his seagoing ancestors Harold somehow kept the course and just before ten o'clock, in impenetrable darkness, we arrived at Muddy Hole.

I had to take his word for it. The twin cones of the headlights revealed nothing but rain and fog. Harold rushed me from the car and a moment later was pounding on an unseen door. It opened to allow us to enter a tiny, brilliantly lit, steaming hot kitchen where I was introduced to the

brothers Mike and Paddy Hallohan. Dressed in thick home-spun sweaters, heavy rubber boots and black serge trousers they looked like a couple of characters out of a smuggling yarn by Robert Louis Stevenson. Harold introduced me explaining that I was the "mainland feller" who had come to see their boat.

The brothers wasted no time. Rigging me up in oilskins and a sou'wester they herded me out into the storm.

The rain beat down so heavily that it almost masked the thunder of breakers which seemed to be directly below me, and at no great distance away.

" 'Tis a grand night fer a wreck!" Paddy bellowed cheer-fully.

It was also a grand night to fall over a cliff and break one's neck; a matter of more immediate concern to me as I followed close on Paddy's heels down a steep path that was so slippery your average goat would have thought twice about attempting it. Paddy's storm lantern, fuelled for economy reasons with crude cod-liver oil, gave only a symbolic flicker of light through a dense cloud of rancid smoke. Nevertheless the smoke was useful. It enabled me to keep track of my guide simply by following my nose.

Twenty minutes later I bumped heavily into Paddy and was bumped into as heavily by Mike who had been following close behind. Paddy thrust the lamp forward and I caught a maniacal glimpse of his gnome-like face, streaming with rain and nearly split in two by a gigantic grin.

"Thar she be, Skipper! T'foinest little bummer on t'South-ern Shore o' Newfoundland!"

I could see nothing. I put out my hand and touched the flank of something curved and wet. Paddy shoved the lantern forward to reveal reflections from the most repellent shade of green paint I have ever seen. The colour reminded me of the naked belly of a long-dead German corpse with whom I once shared a foxhole in Sicily. I snatched my hand away.

Mike roared in my ear. "Now dat you'se seen her, me dear man, us'll nip on back to t'house and have a drop o' tay."

Whereupon Mike and Paddy nipped, leaving me stumbling anxiously in their wake.

Safely in the kitchen once more I found Harold had never left that warm sanctuary. He later explained that he had felt it would have been an intrusion for him to be present at my first moment of communion with my new love. Harold is such a thoughtful man.

By this time I was soaked, depressed, and very cold; but the Hallohan brothers and their ancient mother, who now appeared from a back room, went to work on me. They began by feeding me a vast plate of salt beef and turnips boiled with salt cod which in turn engendered within me a monumental thirst. At this juncture the brothers brought out a crock of Screech.

Screech is a drink peculiar to Newfoundland. In times gone by it was made by pouring boiling water into empty rum barrels to dissolve whatever rummish remains might have lingered there. Molasses and yeast were added to the black, resultant fluid and this mixture was allowed to ferment for a decent length of time before it was distilled. Sometimes it was aged for a few days in a jar containing a plug of nigger-twist chewing tobacco.

However the old ways have given way to the new, and Screech is now a different beast. It is the worst conceivable quality of Caribbean rum, bottled by the Newfoundland government under the Screech label, and sold to poor devils who have no great desire to continue living. It is not as powerful as it used to be but this defect can be, and often is, remedied by the addition of quantities of lemon extract. Screech is usually served mixed with boiling water. In its consequent near gaseous state the transfer of the alcohol to the bloodstream is instantaneous. Very little is wasted in the digestive tract.

This was my first experience with Screech and nobody had warned me. Harold sat back with an evil glitter in his eye and watched with delight as I tried to quench my thirst. At least I *think* he did. My memories of the balance of that evening are unclear.

At a much later date I was to be accused by Jack of having bought our boat while drunk, or of having bought her sight unseen, or both. The last part of the accusation is certainly not true. As I sat in the overwhelming heat of the kitchen with steam rising to maximum pressure inside my own boilers, the brothers Hallohan drew on the wizardry of their Irish ancestors and conjured up for me a picture of their little schooner using such vivid imagery that I saw her as clearly as if she had been in the kitchen with us. When I eventually threw my arms around Paddy's neck and thrust a bundle of bills into his shark-skin textured hand, I knew with sublime certainty that I had found the perfect vessel.

As we drove back to St. John's the next morning Harold rhapsodized about the simple-hearted, honest, God-fearing Irish fishermen of the Southern Shore.

"They'd give you their shirt as soon as look at you," he said. "Generous? Migod, there's nobody in the whole world like them! You're some lucky they took to you."

In a way I suppose Harold was right. Because if the Hallohans had not taken to me I might have remained in Ontario where I could conceivably have become a solid citizen. I bear the Hallohans no ill will, but I hope I never again get "took to" the way I was taken on that memorable night at Muddy Hole.

Two days later I returned to Muddy Hole to do a survey on my vessel and to get my first sober (in the sense of calm, appraising) look at her. Seen from a distance she was indeed a pretty little thing, despite her nauseous colour. A true schooner hull in miniature, she measured thirty-one feet on deck with a nine-foot beam and a four-foot draft. But she was rough! On close inspection she looked as though she had been flung together by a band of our paleolithic ancestors – able shipbuilders perhaps but equipped only with stone adzes.

Her appointments and accommodations left a great deal to be desired. She was flush-decked, with three narrow fishing wells in each of which one man could stand and jig for cod, and with two intervening fish holds in each of which the ghosts of a million long-dead cod tenaciously lingered.

Right up in her eyes was a cuddy two feet high, three feet wide, and three feet long, into which one very small man could squeeze if he did not mind assuming the foetal position. There was also an engine room; a dark hole in which lurked the enormous phallus of a single-cylinder, make-and-break (but mostly broke) gasoline engine.

Her rigging also left something to be desired. Her two masts had apparently been manufactured out of a couple of Harry Lauder's walking sticks. They were stayed with lengths of telephone wire and cod line. Her sails were patched like Joseph's coat and seemed to be of equivalent antiquity. Her bowsprit was hardly more than a mop handle tied in place with netting twine. It did not appear to me that the Hallohans had sailed her very much. I was to hear later that they had *never* sailed her and shared the general conviction of everyone in Muddy Hole that any attempt to do so would probably prove fatal.

She was not a clean little vessel. In truth, she stank. Her bilges had not been cleaned since the day she was built and they were encrusted with a glutinous layer of fish slime, fish blood, and fish gurry to a depth of several inches. This was not because of bad housekeeping. It was done "a-purpose" as the Muddy Holers told me *after* I had spent a solid week trying to clean her out.

"Ye see, Skipper," one of them explained, "dese bummers now, dey be built o' green wood, and when dey dries, dey spreads. Devil a seam can ye keep tight wit' corkin (caulking). But dey seals dersel's, ye might say, wit' gurry and blood, and dat's what keeps dey tight."

I have never since had reason to doubt his words.

Since the sum the Hallohans had demanded for their vessel was, oddly enough, exactly the sum I had to spend, and since this nameless boat (the Hallohans had never christened her, referring to her only as She, or sometimes as That Bitch) was not yet ready to go to Samoa around Cape Horn, I had to make a serious decision.

The question really was whether to walk away from her forever, telling Jack McClelland a suitable lie about having been waylaid by highwaymen in St. John's, or whether to try and brazen it out and somehow make a vessel out of a sow's ear. Because I am essentially a coward, and anyway Jack is onto my lies, I chose the latter course.

Upon asking the Hallohans where I could find a boatbuilder who could make some necessary changes for me I was directed to Enarchos Coffin – the very man who had built the boat four years earlier. Enos, as he was called, was a lean, lank, dehydrated stick of a man. In his younger days he had been a master shipwright in Fortune Bay building vessels for the Grand Banks fishery, but when the Banking fleet faded into glory he was reduced to building small boats for local fishermen. The boats he built were beautifully designed; but a combination of poverty amongst his customers, a shortage of decent wood, failing vision, and old age, somewhat affected the quality of his workmanship. The Hallohan boat was the last one he had built and was to be the last he would ever build.

When I went to visit him, armed with an appropriate bottle, he was living in a large, ramshackle house in company with his seven unmarried daughters. Enos proved amiable and garrulous. The Southern Shore dialect is almost unintelligible to the ear of an outsider and when it is delivered at a machine-gun clip it becomes totally incomprehensible. For the first hour or two of our acquaintance I understood not a single word he addressed to me. However after the first burst of speed had run its course he slowed down a little and I was able to understand quite a lot.

He said he was delighted to hear I had bought the boat; but when he heard what I had paid for her, he was only able to cure his attack of apoplexy by drinking half the bottle of rum, neat.

"Lard livin' Jasus!" he screeched when he got his breath back. "An' I built her for they pirates fer two hunnert dollars!"

At which point I snatched the bottle from him and drank the other half of it, neat.

When we had recovered our breath I asked him if he would undertake repairs, modifications, and a general refit. He willingly agreed. We arranged that he would fit a false keel and outside ballast; a cabin trunk over the fish wells; bunks, tables, lockers, and other internal essentials; re-spar, re-rig her properly, and do a hundred other smaller but necessary jobs. Enos thought the work would take him about two months to complete.

I returned to St. John's and thence to Ontario in moderately good spirits. I did not worry about the boat being ready on time, since we did not plan on sailing her until mid-summer. Occasionally I wrote to Enos (he himself could neither read nor write) and one or other of his strapping daughters would reply with a scrawled postcard of which this one is typical:

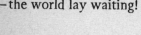

Dear Mister Mote
  Dad say yor boat come fine lots fish
  this month Gert got her baby
                        Nellie Coffin

During the waiting months Jack and I dreamed many a dream and made many a plan. We agreed that I should precede him to Newfoundland near the end of June taking with me a jeep-load of gear and equipment, and that I would have the few finishing touches to the boat completed so that she would be ready to sail when Jack arrived in mid-July. After that, well, we would see. Bermuda, the Azores, Rio de Janeiro – the world lay waiting!

2 · "Passion Flower" goes to sea

Jack McClelland was not the only man who owned a surrogate ship in which he could perform deeds of derring-do when life became unbearable. His little launch *cum* motor torpedo boat on Lake Muskoka was matched by a vessel I had owned for ten long years. To uninitiated eyes she seemed none other than a singularly decrepit jeep station wagon; but in the reality of imagination she was the last of the square-riggers trading between London and Ceylon.

To add authenticity to her assumed character she carried oil-burning running-lights, green to starboard, red to port, on the sides of her wheelhouse. On her bows she mounted a wench (seaman's parlance for winch) with forty fathoms of cable. She had no figurehead but on bow and stern she carried her name, her port of registry, and her motto.

PASSION FLOWER
4th. Concession Of Albion Township
Do Or Die

Many is the time I have sailed her under a full press of canvas down the concession line to Highway 50, then south to pick up the trade winds, and so to the waterfront bars of Toronto. However she had never made a major voyage until the June morning when she and I set out for Newfoundland.

She was as well-prepared for that epochal journey as I could make her. In her capacious hold she carried two Admiralty-pattern anchors (one of 165 pounds and one of 100 pounds). There were three cases of ship's biscuits packed in 1893. There were coils of cordage; bolts of sailcloth; cork life-preservers; a patent log; a compass with a ten-inch card and, as an auctioneer might have said, "other articles too numerous to mention"—which is, in fact, what the auctioneer had said on the April morning when I became his most avid customer.

Passion Flower took her departure from the sand-hills at dawn. A light mist lay over the Albion highlands and a brisk following breeze was waking in the west. It was a marvellous day to begin a great voyage.

For an old vessel she made an amazing passage that first day. With the help of the following breeze, she ran 650 miles of her easting down, and that night I moored her in a green pasture by the side of the St. Lawrence River just east of Quebec City.

I wakened the next morning to the smell of frying bacon. The sun was already up as were the horses in whose pasture I had bivouacked. Off to the north the great silver river rolled towards the still-distant sea, and to the south the horses formed a silent semi-circle around *Passion Flower*, me, and a stranger to my ken.

He was a small wrinkle-faced, scraggly-bearded fellow of indeterminate age dressed in worn serge trousers, a frayed shirt and a canvas jacket. I sat up in my sleeping-bag and stared at him in some astonishment for he was busily engaged in cooking breakfast on *my* gasoline stove, using *my* frying pan, *my* eggs, *my* bacon, and *my* coffee. He saw me move and glanced up.

"Mornin' Sorr," he said politely. "How do ye loik ye're haigs?"

Evidently I had acquired a new crew member during the night. However I had not the vaguest memory of having done so and if my mind was actually giving way I was not prepared to admit it.

"Morning," I replied cautiously. "Sunny side up and lightly done. Coffee black."

"Aye, aye, Sorr. Comin' up."

The mystery solved itself as we were eating.

My new companion, whose name was Wilbur, explained that he was a Newfoundland seaman and that he had been on the road at dawn heading east toward St. John's when he encountered *Passion Flower*. A casual glance through her windows alerted him to the fact that she was a ship disguised as a jeep and so, with the true camaraderie of sailors everywhere, he had welcomed himself aboard.

Wilbur was an acquisition. He had been at sea nearly forty years – or so he said. As we ran eastward that morning along the banks of the mighty river he pointed to many passing ships and told me stories of their crews; stories which, did I dare repeat them in print, would make Henry Miller sound like a purveyor of Victorian nursery rhymes.

Wilbur was a natural raconteur and he never stopped

yarning as we crossed New Brunswick and entered Nova Scotia. By this time I had been ten hours at the wheel and I was weary. When Wilbur offered to take a trick, assuring me that there was not a vessel built he could not steer, I gladly handed over to him.

Gratefully I shut my eyes and slept. Ten minutes later *Passion Flower* brought up all standing with a crash that argued an end to the universe. Wilbur had taken us into a broadside collision with an enormous truck loaded down to her marks with pulpwood logs.

The damage to the two craft turned out to be negligible because *Passion Flower*'s sturdy bow winch had struck an immense tractor tire hanging like a fender over the port side of the truck. The damage to my psyche, to Wilbur's pride, and to the temper of the large man who owned the truck, was not so slight; however this was Nova Scotia and we knew the cure. We sat down, the three of us, in the ditch at the roadside and drank a bottle of rum, after which we parted the best of friends. Both the truck driver and myself were content to accept Wilbur's explanation of what had happened. Ruefully he confessed that while he could steer any vessel that had ever carried sail he had never really learned how to run a motor boat!

I took the wheel. *Passion Flower* now steered in a rather peculiar manner, tracking half-sideways like a crab. Since neither Wilbur nor I possessed much engineering knowledge we did not realize this was because her rudder (landsmen would call it a tie rod or something equally esoteric) was badly buckled. After an hour or two I got used to it but other vehicles approaching us on the road did not. They seemed somewhat uncertain as to our intended course, and not a few of them hauled off the fairway onto the gravel verge to let us pass.

At dusk we found that our electric headlights had also been put out of action by the collision, but since our oil-burning running-lights were trimmed and filled we lit them and were able to proceed, though at reduced speed.

And here I must remark that Nova Scotians, once a famous seafaring race, seem to have lost some of their heritage. At any rate most of the vessels we encountered after dark seemed to understand nothing of the rules of the sea-road. As we bore down upon them, our port lantern flaming red and the starboard flaming green, they sheered off as if they were encountering the *Flying Dutchman*. Some of them were so vocally distressed that I concluded we should anchor for the night, and this we did in the little village of Pugwash.

Once nothing but a lobster-fishing community, Pugwash is now famous for its Thinkers Conferences to which great brains from all the world are welcomed by Cyrus Eaton, an American capitalist. I had heard about this man so I turned *Passion Flower* into the fairway leading to his estate. Mr. Eaton was not in residence, and despite some pretty broad hints from me, the secretary on duty showed no inclination to offer Wilbur and me the hospitality of the place. I lay this rebuff to the fact that I am no capitalist. Just being a thinker was evidently not enough.

We finally moored for the night in the front yard of a lobster fisherman named Angus Mackay, a charming man with a touch of Gaelic in his speech, who took us into his house where his wife fed us to repletion on fried mackerel. Angus also undertook to fix our headlights but the rudder proved beyond his competence.

The next day's voyage was uneventful. Before noon we made Port Hawkesbury on Cape Breton Island where we sought out an old seagoing friend of mine, Harry Langley, from whom we acquired not only fifty fathom of anchor chain (the weight of which made *Passion Flower* squat down until her afterdeck was only inches above the road) but also a case of salt-water soap.

This soap had arrived from overseas in 1887 aboard H.M.S. *Centurion*. *Centurion* is now a rotting hulk lying at the bottom of Sydney harbour but her soap is of more lasting stuff than mere English oak and Swedish iron. Harry assured me I would find no more durable soap anywhere; and he was right. A decade after acquiring that case I am still on the first bar and it may well be another ten years before it softens up to the point where it produces its first lather.

Late that evening we reached North Sydney on the north-east tip of Cape Breton, from which port a car ferry sails over the Cabot Strait to Newfoundland lying ninety miles away across some of the roughest water in the world.

Here I must interrupt the log of *Passion Flower's* voyage to intrude a few words about the great island which was to become so much a part of my life in the months and years ahead. I shall not attempt a new description of it, for one already exists; one which I doubt can be surpassed. I unblushingly plagiarize it. It is from a book called *This Rock Within the Sea* by John de Visser and Farley Mowat.

> *Newfoundland is of the sea. Poised like a mighty granite stopper over the bell-mouth of the Gulf of St. Lawrence, it turns its back upon the greater continent, barricading itself behind the three-hundred-mile-long mountain rampart which forms its hostile western coast. Its other coasts all face towards the open sea, and are so slashed and convoluted with bays, inlets, runs and fiords that they offer more than five thousand miles of shore-line to the sweep of the Atlantic. Everywhere the hidden reefs and rocks (which are called, with dreadful explicitness, "sunkers".) wait to rip the bellies of unwary vessels. Nevertheless these coasts are a true seaman's world, for the harbours and havens they offer are numberless.*
>
> *Until a few generations ago the coasts of the island were all that really mattered. The high, rolling plateau of the interior, darkly coniferous-wooded to the north but bone-bare to the south, remained an almost unknown hinterland. Newfoundland was then, and it remains, a true sea-province, perhaps akin to that other lost sea-province called Atlantis; but Newfoundland, instead of sinking into the green depths, was somehow blown adrift to fetch up against our shores, there to remain in unwill-*

ing exile, always straining back towards the east. Nor is this pure fantasy, for Newfoundland is the most easterly land in North America, jutting so far out into the Atlantic that its capital, St. John's, lies six hundred miles to the east of Halifax and almost twelve hundred miles east of New York.

Mowat's prose may be a little overblown, but essentially his description stands.

The voyage across the Cabot Strait was *Passion Flower's* first encounter with salt water. Shortly before midnight I drove her aboard a huge, slab-sided, unseaworthy monstrosity called *William Carson*, which the Canadian government built to ply the Strait and so link Newfoundland to the rest of the nation. This thing (in truth she cannot be called a vessel) is about as kindly as an old goat with a sore udder; and just about as beautiful. In her swollen belly she carries several hundred cars and trucks, and on this particular evening she was filled to capacity. Each vehicle was secured to mooring rings welded to her decks; although "secured" is perhaps not the word that one should use.

We sailed at midnight. By 0200 hours the *Carson* was wallowing in a heavy beam sea and heaving her great flanks over under the weight of a fifty-mile-an-hour nor'west gale. Her human passengers clung to whatever supports they could find, or rolled about in their bunks moaning an obbligato to the high squeal of the wind. Down below in the vehicle hold all hell broke loose.

The so-called seaman who had made *Passion Flower* fast to the deck must have been a farm boy from Saskatoon, Saskatchewan. Otherwise he would have realized that while four lengths of quarter-inch wire may be enough to moor the insubstantial shell that is your standard North American car, such moorings would be as pack thread to a two-ton jeep, laden with about three tons of assorted ironmongery.

Passion Flower came adrift. At first, so closely were the cars packed, she did not have much room to manoeuvre. But after half an hour she had managed to clear a little space for herself. Each time the *Carson* dropped her heavy snout into a trough, my *Flower* took a run forward to bring up against the stern of a Pontiac owned by a u.s. Air Force captain stationed at Stephenville, Newfoundland. Each time the *Carson* lifted her bows and sagged heavily back on her fat buttocks, *Passion Flower* charged astern, and rammed her towing hook into the grill of a Cadillac belonging to one of the industrial entrepreneurs who were then beginning to make Newfoundland their happy hunting ground at the invitation of Premier Joey Smallwood.

Having somewhat foreshortened these two cars, *Passion Flower* developed enough elbow-room to snap *their* moorings, and then the three of them began charging back and forth together. The chain reaction that followed turned the lower vehicle deck into a shambles that may not have been matched since Claudius Tiberius arranged for three hundred elephants to be stampeded in the Coliseum by forty Nubian lions.

The unloading process at the point of arrival, Port aux Basques, was lively and interesting. The comments of drivers, as they descended to the dock to claim their mutilated vehicles and to arrange for tow trucks, were robust and hearty.

Although she looked as if she had been on ice-breaking duty for several months, *Passion Flower* drove off the ferry under her own power. Apparently she had suffered no serious internal injuries. She was, as Wilbur pointed out with no little awe, "still good fer it!"

The five-hundred-and-fifty mile voyage across the centre of Newfoundland was a prolonged exercise in masochism. In those days the Trans-Canada Highway was still a dream existing mainly in the minds of politicians in Ottawa and in St. John's. The reality was so dreadful that nothing but a jeep or an army tank – or a dromedary – could have coped with it. Very few travellers had the temerity to try. Most of them chose to have their vehicles loaded on flat cars at Port aux Basques and shipped by rail to St. John's. I might have done the same had not Wilbur assured me that he had driven the road "t'ousands of toimes," and that there was nothing to it.

He was right. There *was* nothing to it—nothing that could have been called a road. It took us five days to reach St. John's and by then *Passion Flower* was on her last legs. She had blown seven tires; had lost her few remaining springs (her shock absorbers had been absent for years); her muffler; her tail pipe; and her confidence. She staggered into St. John's an old and ailing vessel; but, by God, she got there on her own.

Wilbur left me in St. John's. I asked him where he wished to be put ashore and he directed me to a grey mass of buildings on the city's outskirts. The place looked indescribably gloomy and forbidding.

"Are you sure," I asked, "this is the place you want?"

"Yiss, me son," Wilbur replied happily. "Dat's t'Mental. Dat's t'very place where I belongs!"

It was, too. They met Wilbur at the door and they were as glad to see him as he was to see them. One of them, an intern, I believe, told me about it.

He said Wilbur had been an inmate of the St. John's Mental Hospital for going on twenty years. He never made any trouble; but every now and again he would escape and take a "viyage." In his mind's eye he too was a sailor who sailed the seven seas; but after a few months away he would grow lonely and then he would come home.

Wilbur shook my hand heartily and thanked me kindly.

"Any toime ye needs a mate, ye just calls on me, Skipper!" were his parting words.

And maybe I will; for I have been shipmates with many men I have liked a good deal less.

3· *The sea-green bride*

ALTHOUGH I am very fond of Newfoundland, St. John's is not one of my favourite cities. There is nothing wrong with the physical nature of the place; it is old, pleasantly decrepit, sprawling on steep slopes overlooking a marvellous harbour. Nor do I have any antipathy toward the majority of its people, particularly those who work the vessels at the waterfront, or who, in defiance of the fact that this is a capital city, continue to live and fish as true outporters in a community of straggling houses stuck to the cliffs along the Narrows – the entrance to the harbour.

My dislike of St. John's stems from the fact that it is a parasite. Through at least three centuries it has been a leech squatting behind its high rock portals, sucking the life-blood of the outport people in order to engorge itself. In the early 1960's it still had more millionaires per capita than any other city in North America, including Dallas, Texas. These fortunes were made by remorselessly bleeding the outport fishermen who, until Newfoundland joined Canadian Confederation in 1949, were exploited by the St. John's merchants in a mediaeval fashion. The merchants, whose great warehouses and counting-houses lined Water Street, were called, in helpless bitterness, the "Water Street Pirates." They were the targets for a passive but enduring hatred which they countered by developing a bleak contempt for the people. Totally oriented toward England, they spoke with English accents, sent their children to England to be educated, and were Newfoundlanders in name alone.

The peculiar aroma they gave to the city lingers on and is compounded by a stench of corruption which, while it may not be unique, takes second place to none. Politics in Newfoundland have always been of the Banana Republic – or, to be more accurate, of the Codfish Republic – variety.

Dictatorship has been only thinly disguised under the shabby cloak of threadbare democracy. Some of the most unsavoury figures in North American history have wielded power in St. John's and there is, as yet, no indication that some day the old pattern may be broken.

I did not linger in the city but set out on the Caribou Path along the Southern Shore that very evening. Wheezing and shaking as with palsy, but still game, *Passion Flower* slowly worked her way south through the long night. At dawn she surmounted the last hill behind Muddy Hole and coasted down the rubble slope toward the village. I let her pick her own way among the boulders and gave my attention to the scene below.

The little harbour, a mere slit in the crooked coastal cliffs, lay quiescent in the pearl-blue light of early morning. Thirty or forty open boats slumbered at their moorings like a raft of sleeping eiders. A ramshackle filigree of fish flakes (racks for drying fish), wharves, stages, and fish stores patterned the shores of the cove in grey and silver. Two-score square, flat-roofed houses painted in garish colours clambered up the slope from the landwash. Directly below me sprawled the fish plant, a drift of oily smoke rising from its stark, iron chimney.

It was a somnolent, gentle scene and of a piece with the rest of the thirteen hundred Newfoundland outports which in those days still clung, as they had clung for centuries, to the convoluted coast of the great island. I took in the scene with a pleasure that slowly changed to anxiety.

Something was missing – and that something was my dream ship. She should have been lying in the harbour below me, bobbing gently at her moorings, alert and lovely, and waiting like a bride for her lover to come. The lover *had* come – was here, was now – but of the sea-bride there was not a trace.

Passion Flower butted her way through the last rocky barricade on the goat track leading down to the fish plant, hiccuped once or twice and quietly expired. When I tried to start her again she only whined piteously. I climbed out and was confronted by a very small boy who seemed to spring like one of the Little People out of the rock-strewn slope. He was a towhead, with rubber boots several sizes too large, a runny nose, and a shy smile. I asked him where I could find Uncle Enos Coffin (in the outports men over fifty are almost invariably called uncle by their juniors), and he pointed up the hill to a large house painted in wide horizontal stripes of puce, canary yellow, and Pompeian red.

I must digress a moment to remark that until Confederation few outport Newfoundlanders could afford to buy paint. They made their own out of ochre earth mixed with cod-liver oil and sea water. When dry (and that might take a year), it looked like old blood. It was hardly an exciting hue, and over the centuries the outport people became colour starved. Soon after the island became part of Canada it was inundated by carpetbaggers from the mainland, amongst whom were a number of paint salesmen. It was also inundated with cash money as a result of the federal baby bonus and old-age pension plans. Much of this money was promptly exchanged for paint. Drunk with colour, many outporters were not content to paint their houses red, or grass green, or boudoir pink – they painted them varicoloured with horizontal, vertical, and even diagonal stripes. Viewed from several miles to seaward on a foggy day the effects were visually pleasing. Viewed from close at hand on a sunny day the effect was one to make strong men quail.

"Thank you," I said. "Now, would you know where the schooner is that used to belong to the Hallohans?"

The boy's face lit up. He turned and shuffled off between two decayed warehouses and I followed. We emerged at the base of a spindly and unbelievably rickety stage (as fishermen's wharves are called) made of peeled spruce poles.

Lying alongside it was a boat.

The tide was out and she lay on her side, half in the water and half out of it, amidst a rich collection of broken bottles, rotting kelp, dead fish, and nameless slimy objects. I picked my way out along the cod-oil soaked sticks of the stage and stood beside my dream ship.

Her hull had not been touched since I had seen her last and the remains of her green paint hung in scrofulous tatters from her naked planking. Her belly, bare of the last trace of copper paint and smeared with bunker oil, gleamed greasily. Her decks were a patchwork of gaping holes, open seams, rough pieces of new plank, and long black rivulets of tar, where someone had been doing some perfunctory caulking. Her mainmast was broken off ten feet above the deck and her foremast, unstayed, swayed at a weird angle importuning the unheeding skies.

The most appalling thing about her was an enormous unpainted box-like structure that appeared to have been roughly grafted to her decks. It was huge, stretching from the steer-

ing-well forward to the foot of the foremast. It looked like a gigantic sarcophagus. It was as if the little ship, feeling herself to be dying of some incurable and loathsome disease, had taken her own coffin on her back and gone crawling off to the graveyard, but had not quite been able to make it and had died where she now lay.

The sight of her left me speechless, but it had the opposite effect on my snuffy-nosed little guide. He spoke for the first time.

"Lard Jasus, Sorr!" he said. "Don't she be a wunnerful quare sight?"

I did not immediately seek out Enos because, although I am a peaceable man, there was murder in my heart. Instead I climbed back into *Passion Flower*, and, as I am wont to do when faced with difficult situations, I opened a bottle.

My major preoccupation at that moment was with Jack McClelland. Jack was due to arrive in Muddy Hole in two weeks to begin our cruise. Jack is one of the Golden People who have but little understanding of the frailties of ordinary mortals. He is A Man Who Gets Things Done, and he expects those with whom he deals to be equally efficient. He does not supplicate the Fates, he gives them orders. He gives *every-body* orders, and he had given me mine.

"On July fifteenth, at 0730 hours, we will sail from New-foundland for the nearest palm-fringed islet, where we will spend the summer giving ourselves over to the pleasures of a hedonistic existence. Is that clearly understood?"

Such were his parting words to me. I was reasonably sure he would not be content to spend the summer in Muddy Hole.

After my first suck at the bottle I still thought I might stave in Enos Coffin's skull, plead insanity, and get myself committed to the St. John's Mental where Wilbur and I could keep each other company until Jack forgot about me. After two more sucks, I determined to get *Passion Flower* under way and steam off to a place I know about on the Yukon-Alaska border, where there is a lot of archaeological work to be done on the antiquity of early man in North America. However *Passion Flower* absolutely refused to start, so I took another suck or two and concluded that I would stay where I was for the nonce and seek a more direct route to oblivion.

Enos Coffin's seven hearty daughters found me there when they came galumphing along to start the morning shift at the fish plant. They were good, understanding girls. One of them rested my head in her ample lap while another went off to find Enos. Later the group of them escorted me, which is to say they carried me, up to their house where they put me contentedly to bed.

I wakened late that evening in no good humour. But Enos's daughters were so hospitable and lavished so much attention on me (including an immense feed of fried cod's tongues and cod's cheeks), that I did not speak as harshly to Enos as he deserved. To my complaint that he had betrayed me, he replied in tones of injured innocence:

"Why didn't ye tell I ye was in such a hurry for the boat? If I'd a know'd I'd a had her done up mont's ago. But don't you be worryin' none, me darlin' man. I'll get right aholt of Obie Murphy an the two of we'll have her ship-shape afore the week is out. And oh, Skipper, ye don't happen to have anudder bottle wid ye, do ye? I finds me stomach something turrible those days!"

Since, as it happened, I was also finding my stomach "something turrible," I located another bottle and before the night ended I too was full of optimism.

Now if there is one salient quality native to outport New-foundlanders, it is optimism. They really need it. Without it, they would long ago have had to turn their island back to the gulls and the seals. With it they accomplish miracles. Given sufficient optimism they are the ablest, most enduring and the most joyful people on this earth.

When Enos and Obie Murphy (an amiable fisherman of gargantuan strength) started work on the boat the next

day, it became my chief task to keep them supplied with optimism. In order to do this, I had to establish a regular run between Muddy Hole and St. John's, the nearest place where optimism could be procured. I would start off for the city in the early morning, reach it late in the afternoon, have the jeep repaired, try to buy such vital articles for the boat as sails, pumps, etc. (more of this later), and I would pick up a gallon or two of optimism from the bootleggers, who sold a better and cheaper product than did the government-owned liquor stores. I would then drive all night, reaching Muddy Hole in time to prepare Enos and Obie for the day's work which lay ahead of them.

As time passed the navigation of the caribou track became less of an ordeal. *Passion Flower* gradually wore down the worst of the boulders and chewed up most of the stumps. By the time she made her final trip, the path had become enough like a road to prompt the residents of the Southern Shore to an act of gratitude. They petitioned the government to have the trail named "Passion Flower Passage." The government might have done it too except that the Premier, Mr. Joey Smallwood, was afraid that once he had acknowledged the road's existence he would have to maintain it.

One reason I did not mind making these long voyages was that the alternative, helping Enos and Obie work on the boat, was too terrible to contemplate. I avoided contemplating it for several days, until Enos began fitting a false keel and two thousand pounds of iron ballast. An extra pair of hands was needed then and I had to supply them. To give the flavour of the working conditions I can do no better than refer to my notes made at the time.

The boat was lying in a tiny slip dominated by the fish plant. All the effluence, both human and animal, from this plant, which employed one hundred and forty-seven men, women and children, and which processed about 100,000 pounds of fish a day, was voided into our slip through a ten-inch sewage pipe that vomited at us at irregular intervals. At low tide, the pallid guts of defunct codfish formed a slippery pattern all about the boat and festooned all her lines. The air, already pretty noxious, was further poisoned with gases from the meal plant. Such fish offal as was not poured into the water was reduced to stinking yellow powder that sifted down from heaven upon our bared heads, like the debris from a crematorium. So awful was the stink that four wooden barrels standing at the end of the stage, wherein Obie was wont to throw the livers of newly caught codfish, so they could rot and reduce to oil under the heat of the sun, gave off a rather pleasant fragrance by comparison. Our clothing, bodies, hair, became slimy with the effluvium of long-dead cod and, of course, every inch of the vessel was thickly coated with . . . .

It was a situation where a man needed all the optimism he could get!

However not even all the optimism in Newfoundland could enable us to accomplish the impossible, and as the day of Jack's arrival drew nearer I was forced to admit to myself that the little ship was not going to be ready to sail on schedule.

By July tenth she still lacked spars, rigging, sails, a propeller, and a variety of other vital items. She also lacked sufficient pumps. Late on the evening of the tenth we finished paying her seams and painting her bottom and at high tide hauled her to the head of the wharf. She immediately proceeded to give evidence of what was to be her most salient characteristic. She leaked as no boat I have ever known, before or since, *could* leak.

The water did not seem to enter from any particular place, but to come in by some arcane process of osmosis through every pore. It was necessary to pump her every hour, on the hour, and in between the hours, just to keep abreast of the inflow. There was no question of getting ahead of it since there were only three of us and we could only operate three pumps at a time.

The little schooner's apparent desire to commit hara-kiri did not bother Enos or Obie. From Enos I heard a phrase which was to echo like an eternal whisper in my ears throughout the next several years.

"Southern Shore boats all leaks a drop when they first lanches off," Enos told me soothingly. "But once they's been afloat a day or two, *why they takes up*."

Like most things Enos told me there was truth in this. Southern Shore boats *do* take up. They take up unbelievable quantities of salt water, and they take up most of a man's time just working at the pumps. The fantastic arm and shoulder musculature of Southern Shore fishermen is sufficient testimony to this.

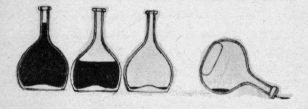

4· *Farillon and Ferryland*

T HE HELLISH days I spent in Muddy Hole and in St. John's might well have proved unendurable had it not been for the Morry family of Ferryland.

Ferryland lies not far from Muddy Hole but, unlike its sister outport, it remains habitable by reason of the fact that it does not have the dubious blessing of a fish plant.

My presence and purpose at Muddy Hole soon became known in Ferryland as indeed it was known along the whole Southern Shore. One day when she was bounding back from St. John's *Passion Flower* had a conniption fit, snorted horribly a few times, and took a fainting spell outside the white-painted picket fence enclosing a big old house on Ferryland's outskirts.

I went up to the house to ask for help and was met at the door by Howard Morry. Before I could open my mouth to speak he forestalled me.

"Come you in, Mister Mowat," he boomed. "Come you in and have a cup of tay."

Howard was then in his eightieth year but I took him to be a man of fifty. Tall, firmly joined, heavy set, with a rubi-cund and unlined face, he was the epitome of a farmer-fisherman from Drake's time. He was a widower living with his rangy and laconic son Bill, and his voluble daughter-in-

33

law Pat. Bill and Pat ran a small store and a small salt-fish-making industry. They had two charming children, a boy and a girl.

The Morrys seemed to know what I was undergoing at Muddy Hole and took it on themselves to provide an antidote. From that first meeting until I sailed away their home was mine. Pat fed me fantastic meals, bullied the hell out of me, and saw to it that I seldom went to bed sober. Bill made me a part of the ancient fishing pattern of the harbour, sending me out with the trap boat crews, showing me the arts and secrets of making salt fish, and subjecting me to his own fierce, unyielding belief in the importance of human continuity in all things. Young Peter Morry, age ten, took me on long, secret walks into the "country" over trails made by the Masterless Men and up to the high places like the Gaze, a long hillcrest from which, for centuries, women watched for the returning ships, or men stood guard to cry the alarm when pirate sails hove over the horizon.

However it was Howard Morry who truly took me into the heart and soul of Newfoundland and Newfoundlanders. Howard was one of those rare people whose feeling for the past amounted to an intense and loving intimacy. His great-great-grandfather had been the first Morry to reach the Southern Shore, and all the tales that had come down the long ladder of the generations had finished up in Howard's head – and in his heart.

During his middle years he suffered a severe accident and had to lie a-bed for twenty months. He used this time to transcribe every memory of Ferryland he had ever heard into thirty school scribblers. When he was well again, and back at sea and at his trade, he negligently tossed this priceless treasure into a corner where some children found it and used the books to make a bonfire. When Howard told me about this incident, I was appalled. He only chuckled. " 'Twas of no account. I still have every word of it written in me head."

Howard not only knew the story of Ferryland during his own family's time but he knew it, or felt it, as far back as history can go. That was a long way back since Ferryland is one of the places in Newfoundland where the patina of human occupation is thick enough to really soften the bony face of the old Rock.

The broad and well-protected harbour lying at the foot of low, swelling hills, fringed by a wide foreshore of grassy meadows, welcomed some of the earliest European visitors to North America. Basque whalers and cod fishers sheltered in Ferryland harbour well before the end of the fifteenth century. During the first decades of the sixteenth century Bretons and Normans had fishing stations along its beaches. It appears on an old French chart of 1537, as Farillon. Yet the French must have come late upon the scene for this name was not of their bestowal. Even then it was a corruption of an earlier name.

The French held Farillon as a permanent settlement until it was seized from them by English pirates about 1600. In

1621 Lord Baltimore chose it as the site of a grandiose plantation scheme he had proposed for Newfoundland. However, the Lord was hag-ridden. His wife could not stand Firiland, as it was then called, and two years later persuaded her master to shift south to what became the State of Maryland.

Over the succeeding centuries other overlords usurped nominal control of the place and sweated the inhabitants. But its people, of mixed French, West Country English, Jersey, and Irish stock went on about their business with the sea, paying very little heed to those who rode upon their shoulders. Tough, stubborn, infinitely enduring, they survived the black years of the Fishing Admirals when English kings bowed to the demands of powerful fishing interests in the Motherland and decreed that no one could settle in the new land; that it should be kept free of permanent inhabitants; and that it might be used only as a seasonal fishing station by the crews of English ships.

Nevertheless the people of Ferryland held to their home. They held to it through an interminable series of raids by French, New Englanders, Portuguese, and just plain Buccaneers. They held on with the tenaciousness of barnacles. Several times Ferryland had to fight for its life against full-scale naval and military attacks. It survived. It and its people *have* survived through more than four centuries. When I knew it in the early 1960's its nature was not greatly changed from what it must have been at its inception. Howard had innumerable tales to tell that illustrated the nature of the crucible that had formed his people. There was the story of the Masterless Men for example.

During the eighteenth century the English fishing fleet was largely manned by men who had been driven to sea by starvation, or who had been tricked by "recruiters" into making the long, hard voyage across the seas. Having reached Newfoundland many of these men refused to return home again. Treated like slaves by the local "planters" they reacted like Spartan slaves and fled from the little harbours into the desolate interior. Here they formed a society of their own;

one that endured for a hundred years. They became veritable outlaws in the romantic tradition of Robin Hood, living the forest life and robbing the rich to succour, not only themselves, but also the oppressed fishermen inhabitants of the coast.

The interior of the peninsula became the Country of the Masterless Men. Only the best-armed bands of King's men dared enter their domain. Secret trails ran everywhere, and the villages of the Masterless Men were hidden in a score of deep vales, one of which was within five miles of Ferryland under the loom of a massive hill known as the Butter Pot.

The Masterless Men were never conquered and never subdued; they gradually melded with the coastal settlers and their blood still runs in the veins of the people of the Southern Shore.

Howard Morry brought these men to life again, and others like them, as he took me on little trips along the coast to outports like Bear Cove, La Manche, Admiral's Cove, Cappahayden, Renews, Fermeuse, Aquaforte, Bauline, and other places with equally strange names. Yet Ferryland remained the heart of his love.

One afternoon he took me out to Bois Island which lies in the broad mouth of Ferryland harbour. Once it was well wooded, but that was in distant days. Now no trees grow on it and it is a place of fantasy.

Forgotten or ignored by official historians, familiar only to a handful of men like Howard, it is a great fortress. Around its almost sheer perimeter is an earthwork circumvallation. At least five heavy gun batteries still lie emplaced at intervals, the muzzles of the guns showing black and stark through a guanoed growth of mosses. Magazines, the ruins of dwelling houses, and even an ancient well can still be traced. According to Howard it was first fortified before 1600 by the French. By 1610 it had been taken by the English super-pirate Peter Easton and was gradually improved until it became an almost impregnable structure and the key to Ferryland's long survival.

In shoal water at the foot of a great crevice lay four corroding, twenty-pound, long guns of the seventeenth century, just as they had been left when an eighteenth-century privateer attempted to steal them from the temporarily abandoned fort. Nothing else appeared to have been disturbed since the fort last lived. Here were no guides, no gravel paths, no fanciful reconstructions. Here was the true reality of the past; dimmed only and not obliterated by the flickering centuries.

With the passing of men like Howard Morry (and they are all too few in any land) most of the rich and vital human past of Newfoundland will have gone beyond recall. And a way of life four centuries old will have vanished.

I count myself lucky I had a chance to taste that way of life—the way of the cod fisher. One morning at four o'clock Howard woke me from a down-filled bed, fed me a whopping breakfast, and took me through the darkness to the stage head where I was to join the four-man crew of a trap boat.

She was a big, broad-beamed skiff powered by a five-horsepower, "jump spark," single-cylinder engine. It was calm and cold as we puttered out of the harbour accompanied in darkness by the muted reverberations from a score of other "one-lungers" pushing unseen boats toward the open sea.

Our crew had two cod traps to examine. Essentially

these traps are great boxes of netting as much as fifty feet on a side. They have a bottom but no top. Stretching out from a "door" on one side is a long, vertically hung leader-net to guide the slow moving cod into the trap. The whole affair is moored to the sea floor with huge wrought-iron anchors which are the last surviving artifacts of ancient and forgotten ships.

Our first trap was set in nine fathoms off Bois Island and we reached it just at dawn. While the rest of us leaned over the side of the skiff, staring into the dark waters, our skipper tested the trap with a jigger – a six-inch leaden fish equipped with two great hooks, hung on the end of a heavy line. He lowered the jigger into the trap and hauled sharply back. On the first try he hooked a fine fat cod and pulled it, shimmering, aboard.

"Good enough!" he said. "Let's haul her, byes."

So haul we did. Closing the trap mouth and then man-handling the tremendous weight of twine and rope took the best efforts of the five of us and it was half an hour before the trap began to "bag," with its floats upon the surface. As we passed armloads of tar-reeking, icy twine across the gunwales, the bag grew smaller and the water within it began to roil. We had a good haul. The trap held twenty or thirty quintals* of prime cod seething helplessly against the meshes.

One of our number, a young man just entering his twenties, was working alongside the skiff from a pitching dory. He was having a hard time holding his position because of a big swell running in from seaward. An unexpected heave on the twine threw him off balance, and his right arm slipped between the dory and the skiff just as they rolled together. The crack of breaking bones was clearly audible. He sat back heavily on the thwart of his dory and held his arm up for inspection. It was already streaming with blood. A wristwatch, just purchased and much treasured, had been completely crushed and driven into the flesh.

The injured youth lost hold of the net and his dory was fast driving away from us on the tide rip. Our skipper cried out to us to let go of the trap while he started the engine, but the young man in the drifting dory stopped us.

"Don't ye be so foolish!" he shouted. "I'se able to care for myself! Don't ye free them fish!"

Using his good arm, he swung an oar over the side and hooked an end of the header rope with it, then with one hand and his teeth he pulled himself and the dory back to the skiff along the rope. We took him on board, but he would not let us leave the trap until every last cod had been dip-netted out of it and the skiff was loaded down almost to her gunwales. During all this time, perhaps twenty minutes, he sat on the engine hatch watching us and grinning, as the blood soaked the sleeve of his heavy sweater and ran down his oilskin trousers.

*A quintal is the ancient and traditional measure used by the cod fishers. It is equal to 112 pounds, dry weight, of salt fish.

When we got back to the stage it was ten o'clock and the sun was high and hot. Pat Morry met us with a truck and we took the lad away to the doctor who set the bones and took sixteen stitches to close the wound. I went along and as we left the doctor's little office the young man said to me;

"Skipper, I hopes I never spiled yer marnin'!"

No, he did not "spile" my morning. But how was I to find words to tell him what kind of a man I knew him to be? He would have been dreadfully embarrassed if I had tried.

Whenever I stayed at the Morrys' overnight I would go to the stage head the following morning to welcome the trap boats home. Invariably I would be joined there by Uncle Jim Welch and Uncle John Hawkins. They were eighty-eight and ninety years old respectively. Both had been fishermen all their lives but, as Uncle John put it, "We's just a mite too old for that game now, bye. No good fer it no more." Nevertheless they were still good enough to check each boat, to make acid comments on the quality and quantity of the fish, and to keep the "young fellers" (men of forty and fifty) up to the mark. Uncle John first went to sea in a dory, jigging fish with his father, at the age of eight. He was a late starter. Uncle Jim began *his* fishing career at the age of six.

The individual stories Howard Morry had to tell were legion and they were a blend of the comic and the tragic, for that is the blend of ordinary life. One evening we were talking about the priests along the coast (the Southern Shore is almost exclusively Roman Catholic) and Howard told me the tale of Billard and the goat.

Everybody on the Southern Shore grew potatoes and Billard was particularly proud of his patch. Unfortunately one of his neighbours kept goats, and goats like potatoes too. One morning Billard was harvesting his spuds, back bent, eyes on the peaty ground, when the priest happened by. The Father paused, leaned on the fence and asked:

"Are ye diggin' 'em, Billard?"

Billard glanced out under his bushy eyebrows, failed to see the priest, and met, instead, the amber stare of a particularly outrageous billy-goat peering through another section of the fence.

"Yiss, ye whore!" answered Billard fiercely. "And if 'twasn't fer you, there'd be a lot more of 'em!"

The same evening Howard told me a different kind of tale. A hundred and seventy years ago a middle-aged man appeared in Ferryland. He was a runaway from a fishing ship, an "Irish Youngster"—the name given to the men and boys of any age who, fleeing starvation in Ireland, indentured themselves to the English fishing fleet and the Newfoundland planters.

Ferryland people took him in and made him welcome but he was a haunted man—"afeard." He was convinced he would be recaptured and returned to servitude. He stayed in the settlement for a few months, took a young girl for wife, and began fishing on his own, but fear never left him. One autumn he took his wife and two babies and rowed away down the coast to a hidden cove which no large ship and few small boats would dare to enter. Here he built a tilt (a tiny wooden cabin) and began living an exile's life.

Once or twice each year he would row into Ferryland to trade his salt fish for essential goods. Then he would disappear again. Apart from these rare trips he, his wife, and his two young sons lived as if they were the only people in the world. They lived from the sea and off the land, catching fish, killing caribou and ducks for meat, and growing a few potatoes in a tiny patch scrabbled out of the moss at the foot of the sea cliffs that guarded them.

One February morning the man was stricken with paralysis. For two weeks his wife nursed him, but he grew worse. Finally she decided she must go for help. She left the boys, aged nine and ten, to care for their father and set out single-handed in a skiff to row thirty or forty miles to Ferryland. It was wicked, winter weather and the pack-ice was particularly bad that year.

She had made fifteen miles when a gale came up and the ice set against the shore, nipping the skiff, and crushing it.

The woman made her way on foot ("copying," they call it) across the floe-ice to the land. She then climbed the ice-sheathed cliffs, swam or waded several small rivers, and eventually fought her way through the snow-laden forest to Ferryland.

It was some time before she recovered enough strength to tell her story; and it was seven long days before the storm, a roaring nor'easter, fell light enough to allow a party of fishermen to make their way along the landward edge of the ice to the distant, hidden cove.

They were met by the two boys; shy to the point of utter silence at this intrusion of strange faces. The men went up to the little house and found it snug and warm and tidy; but the bed was empty. They asked the two boys where their father was and the eldest, the ten-year-old, led them off to a lean-to shack some distance from the cabin. They opened the door and there they found the missing man.

He was strung up to the roof beam by his feet and he had been neatly skinned and drawn.

"You see how it was," Howard explained. "The boys had never looked at human death before. But they had seen a good many deer killed and had watched their father draw and skin them, and so, poor little lads, they thought that must be the right way to treat anything that died, be it man or beast. They did the best they could. . . ."

5· Corsets, cod, and constipation

THE TIME I spent with the Morrys was all too brief. I continued to spend most of my hours, by day and by night, in a mazed struggle to transform a living nightmare into a bearable reality. As the days passed and the work seemed to get no forwarder, I began to feel that Enos and Obie and I were doomed to spend the rest of our lives up to our knees in gurry and frustration. The days slid by–literally *slid*– until one morning the moment of truth was at hand.

The day had come when Jack was due to arrive from Toronto at St. John's airport. The day had dawned when he and the little schooner would come together for the first time.

As I drove *Passion Flower* toward the grey city I was in a subdued and apprehensive mood. However it occasionally happens that the black Fates which haunt our lives feel pity for their victims. There was a considerable amount of fog over the Southern Shore that morning. Since this was the usual state of affairs, I gave it no particular heed. It was not until I had felt my way through St. John's to the airport, there to be told that all flights had been cancelled for several days because of the fog, that I realized I had been reprieved.

I went at once to the forecaster's office. He warmed my heart and brought me joy by predicting that the airport would remain fogbound for some time to come.

"How long?" I asked.

"Difficult to say, old man. Not less than a week, I'd guess."

Feeling positively carefree I wrote a note to Jack explaining that, since there was no phone at Muddy Hole, I would have no way of knowing when he arrived. And, I added, since there remained a certain amount of work to do on the boat, I felt I should not waste time making speculative trips to St. John's on the off chance that Trans-Canada Airlines had managed finally to find the place and effect a landing. I suggested that when he arrived he should rent a small truck (preferably one with four-wheel drive), pick up various items of ship's stores that I had ordered locally, and which I listed for him, and make his own way to Muddy Hole. I left these instructions with a young lady at Trans-Canada's information desk.

Some people may wonder why Jack did not come by rail instead of air, but if any such people there be, they do not know anything about the Newfoundland railroad system.

It is a narrow-gauge railway running five hundred miles, mostly through uninhabited wilderness, from Port aux Basques to St. John's. And it is an antiquity out of another age. Its schedule is so uncertain that under the seats of each coach large wooden boxes are stored. These contain emergency rations for use in case the train is unduly delayed. There are authentic records of the train having taken up to four weeks to cross the island.

The most prolonged delays usually occur during the winter but serious delays can happen at any season for a variety of reasons: fog so thick the engineer cannot see where he is going; rutting bull moose challenging the locomotives to unequal combat (unequal because the moose seldom win); explosions of boilers; windstorms that blow the cars right off the track; temporary loss of passengers who wander off to pick berries while the train is climbing a grade, etc., etc. Not for nothing did Canadian servicemen stationed at St. John's during the war give the train its enduring name—the Newfoundland Bullet.

There have been many poignant happenings aboard the Bullet, but perhaps none holds quite so much pathos as the story of the young lady travelling east from Port aux Basques. As the days drew on she grew increasingly distraught. Every time the conductor passed through her car she would stop him and ask anxiously how much longer the trip would take. He did not know, of course, and eventually he became impatient with her. Why, he asked, was she in such a plunging hurry anyway?

Modestly she told him. She was expecting a baby.

"Ye should have knowed better than to get on the Bullet, and you in this condition!" he told her indignantly.

"Ah, Sorr," she replied, "but I wasn't in this condition when I got on."

Jack McClelland preferred not to take a chance, so he came by air.

I might have guessed that the Fates were only playing with me when they offered a week's respite. The morning after I returned from St. John's I set off with Obie in *Passion Flower* to visit Shoe Cove, some distance down the coast, in hopes of finding spars for the vessel. Just before noon we were both rendered nearly blind by an unexpected burst of sunlight as the fog rolled out to sea. In far away St. John's people stopped in the street to speak to friends they had not seen for many a day, and to stare upward as they heard the unfamiliar thunder of an aircraft's engines.

I have never been able to decide whether I am glad I was not present when Jack arrived at Muddy Hole, or whether my absence should have been a matter for regret. I missed witnessing a scene which has since become part of Southern Shore folklore.

Jack's plane arrived in St. John's at a quarter to one. He disembarked, got my note, and sprang into action. He is like that. He springs into action. On this occasion he did not spring quite as lithely as usual because he had recently put his back "out" and as a consequence was wearing, under his Savile Row sports coat and sharkskin slacks, a fearsome device composed of rubber, steel, and whalebone that would have been the envy of the tightly corseted ladies of the Victorian era.

Nonetheless he sprang to such effect that in less than two hours he was heading for Muddy Hole. Some of the spring went out of him as he drove south, and all of the springs went out of the brand-new, chrome-plated, red-painted convertible Buick which (it was the only such car on the island) he had managed, with his usual ability to overwhelm the better judgement of those he deals with, to rent from St. John's leading garage.

At seven o'clock he arrived at Muddy Hole. The fish plant had just let out, and scores of girls in white aprons and rubber boots, and dozens of men in overalls and rubber boots were pouring out of the stinking building in which they had done their day's servitude. They were stopped in their tracks by the tremendous blare of a tri-tone horn.

At first they thought some strange vessel must be entering the harbour; then one of the girls saw the glint of the setting sun upon a mass of polished chrome poised on the lip of the rocky slope above the settlement.

This was a visitation the likes of which none of the inhabitants of Muddy Hole had ever seen before. As they stared, transfixed, the flame-coloured monster on the crest eased forward over the lip of the descent. *That* galvanized them into action. A hundred arms began to wave as hoarse voices were raised in a great shout.

Jack, at the wheel of the red beast, was delighted.

He thought the people were welcoming him to Muddy Hole. He also thought he was still on the ill-defined track which led down the boulder scree to the shore of the cove.

He was wrong on both counts. There was no road, and the inhabitants were trying vehemently to warn him of this fact.

"My son!" one of the observers of the scene told me afterwards. "It were a wunnerful sight to see!"

And here I had better explain that in Newfoundland the

word "wonderful" still means what it used to mean in older times: full of wonder, full of awe.

The car negotiated the first few yards without incident, then the slope abruptly steepened and although Jack, suspecting by now that all was not well, tramped on the brakes, it was too late. Down came the red behemoth, careless of the boulders in its path and heedless of a number of split-stick fences, leaping and bounding with the abandon of a hippopotamus driven mad by hashish. Things flew out of it. Two thirty-gallon, galvanized tin tanks intended for the boat (one for water and one for fuel) that had been insecurely reposing in the back seat, rose up and described glittering parabolas in the evening air. The trunk flew open, and Jack's modest assortment of seagoing gear, five suitcases and some smaller oddments, abandoned ship.

Suddenly it was all over. The car stood still, its shiny face buried in the end wall of a sheep shed. For a long minute none of the watchers moved. Before they could run to the rescue Jack stepped out of the small dust cloud that hung over the battered shed.

As might be expected of a man who, as commander of a motor torpedo boat, once attempted to make a new entrance into St. John's harbour through a four-hundred foot granite cliff, he had lost nothing of his cool. Blithely he made his way down the remainder of the slope. He was as nonchalant as if he were about to board a luxury cruiser moored to the carpeted docks of the Royal Yacht Club at Cowes.

Enos nervously stepped forward to meet him. He was completely befuddled by the spectacular nature of Jack's arrival. Instead of guiding Jack to his house, pouring him a drink, and holding him there until I returned, Enos obediently responded to Jack's imperious demand that he be taken to the boat at once.

Enos conducted the jaunty and resplendent visitor directly to the stage. Jack took three steps out on the oil-soaked poles, stepped on a putrid piece of cod liver, and his feet went out from under him. Appalled, Enos and three or four other men

leapt *at* him, rather than to him, and in their awkward attempts to help him up—they shoved him overboard.

Although years have fled since then, Jack still refuses to talk about this episode. He claims he cannot remember it at all. I suspect his mental blackout resulted from the ministrations he received that evening from Enos and Enos's seven husky daughters. The strain of spending several hours in an overheated kitchen, being force-fed by a clutch of Valkyries while clad only in a corset and inadequately swathed in a blanket; and while attempting to establish human contact with eight people who seemed to speak no known language, is explanation enough.

Obie and I arrived back at Muddy Hole at midnight. Fortunately Jack was asleep by then. It was with a heavy heart and dubious hopes of the morrow that I crawled into my sleeping-bag.

I was awakened early. Jack stood by my bed wearing a blanket and an anxious look.

"Hi," he said. Then, tautly, "Where in hell's the bathroom?"

Now it is to be borne in mind that Jack is the product of a very good private school, an old Toronto family, and a life of comfort if not of luxury. He is not one of your rough-and-ready pioneering types. He likes his conveniences. He is used to them and he is unhappy without them.

Muddy Hole homes, however, do not boast many conveniences. There are no indoor toilets and there are no outdoor toilets. Ladies keep porcelain pots under their beds but men do not. This seems unfair and, indeed, downright cruel, until one is inducted into the mystery of male behaviour in an outport.

On *my* first visit to Newfoundland it took me several days to resolve this mystery, and I suffered accordingly. However having become a member of the fraternity I was able to spare Jack the agonies of having to find out for himself.

"Hello there. Have a good sleep? Yes? Well, you go on down to the stage; you know, the wharf thing made of sticks. And there's a little shack on the shoreward end of it. It's called the fish store and every fisherman has one. You go inside and you'll find a hole just beside the splitting table, where they dump the cod gurry into the water. And, oh yes, better take some paper with you."

Jack's face was a mirror of the struggle taking place within him. I was touched by the pleading look in his eyes, but it was necessary to be firm.

"Look," I said gently, "you don't have any choice. Not unless you want to try sneaking into the girls' room to borrow the pot." (All seven daughters slept in one room in two beds.) Jack flinched. "And as for the great-out-of-doors, forget it. You'll find yourself entertaining five or six little boys and as many dogs, all of whom will spring full-blown from nowhere as soon as you think you're alone."

Jack moaned a little, gave me a bleak look and headed out the door. He was gone a long time and in his absence the girls got up and lit the fire. By the time he returned they were preparing breakfast.

I felt sorry for Jack, truly sorry. I well remembered my own first visit to a fish store when, perched precariously between wind and water, and surrounded by pungent tubs of codfish soaking in brine, I had injudiciously looked down to behold a consortium of flatfish, sculpins, crabs, and eels staring hopefully upward at me out of the shallows.

Traumatic as the experience must have been, Jack managed to rise above it. But he nearly collapsed when the smell of breakfast struck him. He is a gourmet and a delicate eater. Furthermore he has a weak stomach.

He clutched my arm so hard it hurt and whispered hoarsely in my ear.

"*What* in God's name is *that*?"

"That," I explained cheerfully, "is Newfoundland's national dish. A special treat for visitors. It's called fish-and-brewis."

"Never mind the name. What's *in* it?"

"Well, basically it's a mixture. You take hard bread or ship's biscuits and soak them all night to make them soft and to get rid of the weevils. And you take some shore-dried salt fish and soak *it* all night, 'watering it' is the term. Then you boil the fish and the hard bread and when it's all nice and mushy you pour a cup of spitting hot sowbelly fat over it, and then . . . ."

I never finished my explanation. Jack was already on his way back to visit the sculpins and the eels.

Later that morning when, with the aid of the jeep and several tough but tiny horses, we had extricated the Buick and towed it back to the top of the hill, I felt compelled by some latent trace of honesty to tell Jack the truth about our situation. I explained that even with the best of luck we could not hope to get the boat fit for sea in less than two weeks. I told him that, even then, sailing her would be a most uncertain venture.

"If you want to call it off, Jack, I'd never blame you. Not after what you've been through and, I'd better say it, what you'll have to put up with until we go to sea. You say the word and we'll leave the damned boat lying where she is and head back to St. John's. There's a freighter service running to the Caribbean once a week and the next boat sails tomorrow. We can be aboard her tonight."

Jack was silent for a moment. He looked out across the harbour, past the stages and the fish stores, past the brooding barrier headlands to the grey void of the waiting fog and the dark sea–then to his eternal credit he replied:

"Not a chance! I expect I'll have the worst case of constipation known to medical science. My back is never going to recover from what happened last night. Probably we'll drown when we put out in that fantastic pile of junk you've bought. But, Farley, *we are going to sail her out of here if we both have to die for it.* Now, let's get down to work."

6· *A pounce of pirates*

Jack proceeded to take charge. He concluded that our major problem was lack of organization and the first thing he did was hold a conference in Enos's kitchen. This was attended by Obie, Enos, myself, and an unidentified passerby who said nothing but who spat little geysers of tobacco juice that sizzled on the hot stove top.

In his best board-room manner Jack explained that we had been wasting too much time. The almost daily trips to St. John's were not necessary, he said. Instead, we would make up a detailed list of every item of gear and equipment needed to complete the boat, then he and I would go to the city and in one day of intensive shopping would obtain everything we required.

Upon our return, the four of us, working to a carefully scheduled list of priorities, would pitch in and complete the vessel in a hurry.

"Well, gentlemen, do you agree?" He looked brightly at us for approval.

I looked at Enos, who looked at Obie, who looked at his rubber boots. Nobody said anything. It would have been unkind to have attempted to dampen such innocent enthusiasm.

Jack and I drove to St. John's the next day with the battered Buick in tow behind *Passion Flower*. When we reached

the city we parted, each with his own list, agreeing to meet again at six o'clock at a waterfront bar. Jack took the jeep but I, who had had quite enough experience with the incredible traffic tangles in St. John's, preferred to walk.

I arrived at the bar a little before six. Jack appeared a few minutes later and I hardly recognized him. His blond, usually impeccable hair was a tangled mop. His eyes glared bloodily. There was a spasmodic twitch to his left cheek muscles and his breath was coming and going in sharp, hard whistles.

It required three double rums before he was able to describe his day and then he only told me the highlights. He told of entering shop after shop, most of them empty of customers but full of salesclerks, and of seeing every clerk immediately vanish as if he were the carrier of bubonic plague.

"That's because," I explained sympathetically, "in St. John's it's considered socially demeaning for a clerk to wait on a customer. It isn't done if it can possibly be avoided."

Jack nodded grimly. "That was the least of it. I finally cornered a clerk in a hardware store just as he was making a break for the cellar. I backed him up against a rack of pitchforks and asked him, politely mind you, for five pounds of two-inch nails. And, my God, Farley, you know what he said?" Jack's voice rose to an almost falsetto register. "He said if I would care to leave my order they would try to fill it and I could pick it up next week!"

"You were lucky," I replied soothingly. "Usually they just tell you they don't have what you want, or they may have it next year, or the year after that, or the . . . ."

"But that's not all," Jack interrupted, the twitch in his cheek growing more pronounced. "After searching for two bloody hours I finally found a liquor store and there was actually someone at the counter and I asked him for a case of rum. You know what he did? He made me fill in an application for a special permit and then he sent me to the head office of the Board of Liquor Control to get the permit. It took me an hour to find the place and when I got there everyone was gone for lunch, even though it was half past three. I waited until half past four and finally some scruffy little character came along and told me the goddamn place only processed permits on Wednesdays!"

"That's it, Jack. You see, in St. John's all the store and office people need a lot of rest. It's because they work so hard. But there's another problem too. The merchants have so much money they don't *want* any more. Haven't got any *use* for it. It's an encumbrance to them. You can see how they must feel when a fellow like you comes along and shoves a pile of money at them. Unless they can think fast they might have to take it. Anyway, what *did* you manage to get?"

Jack ground his teeth, thrust his hand into his jacket pocket, fished out a piece of paper and flung it on the table.

It was a parking ticket.

As for me, I had enjoyed a reasonably successful day. Out of the eighty-odd items on my list I had been able to purchase six. They were in a bag at my feet. Six bottles of rum. I had found a bootlegger who was not yet rich, and who didn't mind demeaning himself by dealing with the public. There were not many businessmen like him in St. John's.

Because most of what we needed for the boat was not to be had in St. John's or could not be pried loose from the merchants, we learned to do what outport Newfoundlanders have done for centuries – we improvised. Enos was a master at this. When we needed chain plates for our rigging he got some scrap iron out of an ancient steamship wreck and *cold*

hammered the rusty metal on a rock until he produced four very serviceable sets of plates. Smaller items of hardware he improvised from whatever might be found in the innumerable greasy boxes that cluttered every fisherman's store, and in which, over the generations, every piece of scrap that had ever come to hand had been carefully put by against the hour of future need.

Occasionally we had to go further afield. The cavernous coffin Enos had built over the deck of the schooner was intended as a cabin trunk, but it lacked any means of letting in the light, so that the cabin itself was as dark as the inside of a molasses barrel. After a long search I did find a ship-chandler in St. John's who grudgingly admitted he could supply portlights – at seventy-five dollars each – *if* I was prepared to wait six months until they could be ordered from England. Since I was not so prepared Obie came to the rescue.

Obie had relatives far down the Southern Shore on the Cape Pine Peninsula. Cape Pine is a bleak, forbidding thumb of rock jutting out into the steamer lanes. It is rimmed with reefs and walled against the sea by sheer granite cliffs. It boasts two settlements, two tiny clusters of humanity that somehow cling to the rock walls. How the people make a living seems, at first glance, to be a mystery, for they have no harbours, and it is seldom they can launch their open boats off the tiny beaches because of the tremendous seas that rack those coasts. But the people of St. Shotts and St. Shores (originally St. Jacques and St. Georges) do very nicely. They have gainful employment although they don't talk about it much to strangers. In fact strangers to their coves are not only unwelcome, but may be in some personal jeopardy.

The fact is that the people of St. Shotts and St. Shores have been professional wreckers for generations past. During less constrained times they practised the wrecker's art as a full-time occupation. A vast number of ships fell on their coasts, owing to a lamentable failure on the part of their captains to realize that the light they were steering by was *not* Cape Race (twenty miles to the eastward) but an excellent imitation thereof.

"In death there is life," as a priest upon that shore used to intone as he stood on the cliffs, directing his parishioners in the salvage of cargo from some ship which had foundered with the loss of all hands on the wicked inshore reefs.

Nowadays, of course, the glorious free enterprise practice of using false lights has been curtailed. Nevertheless there are still vessels that make their own fatal errors and end up against the Cape Pine cliffs. Such vessels and their cargo belong, by law, to the underwriters who have insured them, but the people of St. Shotts and St. Shores do not subscribe to this particular law, nor I suspect, to any others either.

Obie and I drove down there in *Passion Flower* and we would never have reached the place in a lesser vessel for there was no road at all most of the way. Our arrival created a sensation. Not only did people peer at us from behind the curtains of every house, but so did the round black eyes of a number of swile guns – long-barrelled, smooth-bore guns intended for killing seals but adaptable to any number of uses.

Obie got out first, was identified, and immediately we were surrounded by masses of hulking great fellows who spoke a language that baffled me completely, even though by then I had developed some skill in dealing with Newfoundland dialects.

However language is not always important. When we off-loaded several bottles of rum we found we were speaking a universal tongue. We stayed the night at St. Shotts, with a brief excursion to St. Shores, and it was all a dream; a magical transportation back through time to a rougher and wilder age. At one point an old woman showed me a small mahogany case crammed with gold coins, some of them of early Spanish vintage. I was told that almost everybody in the two settlements had a similar cache hidden somewhere on the rocky barrens – insurance against the day when modern navigation aids finally deprive these people of their traditional means of making an honest living.

When we headed home the next morning *Passion Flower* was deeply laden. We had eight portlights, one of which was twenty inches in diameter and, with its bronze setting, must have weighed close to a hundred pounds. We also had enough bronze and brass deck and cabin fittings to meet all our needs.

There are those who speak of the St. Shotts people as pirates. Maybe they are. However if it comes to a choice between the pirates of St. Shotts and the pirates of St. John's I know *my* choice.

Most of the residents of the Southern Shore were equally helpful. They and their ancestors had lived for centuries at the mercy of the merchants so they knew exactly what we were up against and they felt for us in our almost continuous need.

Foremost amongst them was Monty Windsor, a soft-spoken, thoughtful man who lived in a rambling house on a tiny, almost insular, peninsula in Aquaforte Harbour. The house had been both imposing and handsome when the Windsors built it nearly two hundred years earlier but it was now grown grey and sad. Monty Windsor was almost the last of that name in Aquaforte. He showed me the family Bible in which were recorded the births and the deaths of generations of Windsors dating back to 1774. Few of the men had died in bed. Most of them perished at sea, some as fishermen, some as sailors, some as whalers, some as privateers. It was a strange old book whose margins had been used for a variety of non-religious, but equally significant purposes.

Inked in a flowery and faded script at the end of Deuteronomy was a recipe for the cure of "throttles" (diphtheria). It called for the patient to smoke a clay pipe loaded with oakum (teased-out strands of tarred hemp rope) which had

first been soaked in brimstone. After smoking this mixture he or she was to swallow a pint of black rum drawn straight from the keg.

Modern medical scientists may scoff, but it seemed self-evident to me that any bacillus or virus that could survive such a treatment would indeed have to be a super-bug. Again, any human being who could withstand the treatment probably had little to fear from germs in any case.

For generations the Windsors had run a whaling factory, a salt-fish plant, and a number of big fishing schooners, but now that was finished and all that remained was a warren of collapsing buildings on the harbour side. These structures held many memories of other ages but they also held treasures for such as us. Here we unearthed a great, two-bladed brass propeller that must have been made half a century earlier but which fitted the shaft of our engine perfectly. We found scores of blocks intended for three-masted schooners and enough smaller blocks to complete our own running rigging. Shackles, belaying pins, mast hoops, sister hooks – in fact, most of what we still needed – were to be found somewhere in the dusty corners of the Windsor buildings.

There remained one requirement that had us stymied. We needed two new spars and they were not to be found. Old masts abounded on the beaches and in the rotting hulls of abandoned schooners, but they were either too big or too old. After four centuries of ship building, wood gathering and forest fires, there was hardly any standing timber left on the Southern Shore. Nothing remained but twisted black spruce scrub – with one exception.

Across the narrow harbour from Monty's house was a stand of almost virgin spruce. It was, in a way, a sacred grove. It had belonged to the family since the arrival of the first Windsor and had been jealously preserved by each succeeding generation as a source of spars, gaffs, and booms for the schooners of the Windsor fleet. Although that fleet had vanished many years earlier, the grove remained sacrosanct. While those trees still stood, undefiled and proud, something of the Windsor heritage remained intact. This, in any case, was how Monty felt about the grove. However when he heard we were having trouble finding spars, he sent a message down to Muddy Hole inviting us to visit him.

We came, Jack and I, and Obie and Enos, and when we reached Monty's house he led us down to a scarred old dory lying on the shore. It was the last vessel of any kind the Windsors owned. There were two axes and some rope lying on the dory's bottom.

"You fellows paddle across to the grove, yonder," Monty told us in his quiet voice. "Climb up the slope a-ways to where you sees a big white rock, and just astern of it you'll find a stand of spruce as straight and true as any on this island. Take what you needs. And make good and sure you gets the best there is."

We did as we were told. Standing on the steep slope, in the odorous shadows of the trees, Enos marked the victims and we cut them down, limbed them, hauled them to the water's edge, and towed them back to the harbour side. I went up to pay Monty for them but he would have none of my money.

"Don't ye be talkin', Skipper. There'll never be need of another one of us cuttin' a stick out of that grove. Likely there'll never be another Windsor go to sea. I'll take it fine to know your little bummer's well spar'd with Windsor wood. It's what those trees was growed to be."

Spit-and-polish yachtsmen may shudder at the thought of anyone cutting down a tree one day and stepping it as a mast two days later with the sap still flowing out of it. Let them shudder. Those spars are still in the vessel as I write and they will last her lifetime, for Newfoundland black spruce, grown on the edge of the ocean, is one of the toughest woods in all the world. However it does have one peculiarity. The grain does not run straight up and down as in trees that grow in more favoured locations. In order to withstand the might of the everlasting gales, shore-grown black spruce grows twisted like a corkscrew or a barber's pole. This gives it great strength but, as the dead tree dries, it tends to unwind. What this meant to us was that both our masts gradually untwisted, turning the crosstrees or spreaders in a circular movement. The cure was simple enough. Every month or two we simply eased off the stays, lifted up the masts, and re-stepped them after giving each a quarter turn. No problem.

The stepping of the masts was a great day at Muddy Hole. To celebrate the occasion Jack made a rapid trip to St. John's and, finding the pettifoggers off their guard, he actually managed to buy a case of rum.

Most Southern Shore Newfoundlanders acquire a taste for rum soon after abandoning their mothers' breasts, and by the time they are grown men they have developed a high degree of immunity to it, but it is not total immunity. Up until this day I had been master of the rum situation and had governed the issuing of rations according to the three cardinal tenets of rum drinking in Newfoundland. The first of these is that as soon as a bottle is placed on a table it must be opened. This is done to "let the air get at it and carry off the black vapours." The second tenet is that a bottle, once opened, must never be restoppered, because of the belief that it will then go bad. No bottle of rum has ever gone bad in Newfoundland, but none has ever been restoppered, so there is no way of knowing whether this belief is reasonable. The final tenet is that an open bottle must be drunk as rapidly as possible "before all t'good goes out of it." Having learned these rules I made it a point never to produce more than one bottle at a time.

Unfortunately Jack did not know the rules and I did not have enough foresight to brief him. When he arrived back from St. John's I was away at the other end of the harbour. He carried the case on board the vessel and lovingly unpacked it, placing all twelve bottles on the saloon table, lined up like twelve little soldiers.

Enos and Obie came below to watch him, and Jack told me later that the ruby glow given off from the bottles, as they sat in a ray of sunshine coming through the forward port-light, was reflected in the oddest manner from the eyes of his two companions.

Jack then went back to the jeep for another load of sup-plies. When he returned to the boat every bottle was open and the corks had vanished. He went on deck to ask Obie about this phenomenon and Obie, wordless as usual, simply pointed to the water of the cove where twelve corks were floating seaward on the receding tide like a child's flotilla.

It was at this moment I returned and at once I realized we had a crisis. Jack was for recorking the bottles with plugs of toilet paper, in lieu of anything better, until I explained that such a departure from tradition would certainly result in a mutiny and might well get us run out of Muddy Hole. The die was cast. There was no turning back; there was only one thing to be done.

"Look," I said in a whisper I hoped would not carry to the deck, "by afternoon every one of those bottles is going to be empty. That is a fact and you can rely on it. And if Enos and Obie do all the emptying there's going to be damn little work done on the boat in the foreseeable future. We just have to sacrifice ourselves, Jack. Start drinking!"

Neither of us are born Newfoundlanders but we did the best we could.

The unclear events of that unclear day can only be hazily reconstructed but one of them stands out. That was when we went ashore to get the new mainmast which Enos had been shaping upon a pair of saw-horses in his front yard. The mast had to be carried about a quarter of a mile down the slope then out on the rickety stage and finally swung into the air and stepped aboard the boat. In preparation for this Obie and Enos went below and when they came on deck there were only eleven little soldiers left on the table. Then the two of them swaggered up to where the mast lay and picked it up, one at each end.

The weight proved a little too much for Enos—it weighed a good three hundred pounds—so Obie shifted to the middle of it, taking the entire strain on his own shoulder, and began to trot down the slope. Obie is a big man and very powerfully built but that mast diminished him until he looked like a small child carrying the biggest caber any Scotsman ever hefted.

Jack and I stood stunned and watched him go. He gained momentum with every plunging step. Enos ran along beside him, a sprightly terrier barking encouragement.

They reached the narrow stretch of level ground at the land-wash and Obie's speed did not diminish. Enos stopped encouraging him and began to yell in a rising inflection:

"Fer Jasus's sake, me son, *slow down!*"

It was no good. Gravity and momentum and various other physical laws which I don't understand had taken full control. Obie went thundering out along the stage—which shook and quivered like a spider's web—and he went right on off the end.

He and the mast made a fantastic splash and the sound brought the girls and the men at the fish plant running to the wharf to see what had happened. They saw Obie astride the mast, laughing like a gawk – a Newfoundland seabird – and paddling toward shore with his big, splayed hands.

That incident established the mood of the day. A dozen men from the plant abandoned their work and came to lend a hand. They fished the mast and Obie out of the soup and then the whole lot of them plunged into the cabin. When they emerged again there had been a slaughter amongst the soldiers but the crowd was now good for anything. They hefted the mast into the air, swung it around by main strength, and dropped it onto its step with such enthusiasm that I expected it to go right through the hull of the boat, skewering her forever to the bottom of Muddy Hole harbour. Then they all went back below for a moment, came out on deck again, picked up the foremast and flung *it* into place. Then they all went below again.

Still trying doggedly to implement our plan Jack and I attempted to get below too but there was no room. When we eventually reached the table there was one bottle still more or less inviolate, so we did our duty.

The centre of activity shifted away from the boat after that. Someone was moved to dig up a can of pure alcohol, smuggled in from St. Pierre, which he had been saving for Christmas. I am told that, late in the day, Enos decided everyone should have a feed of fresh meat – which meant wild meat – and having shouldered a swile gun he disappeared up the slope looking for a caribou. There has not been a caribou within walking distance of Muddy Hole for fifty years, but this was of no moment. Miracles can happen.

None did this time. Instead, Enos lost his precious antique, steel-rimmed glasses somewhere in the scrub woods beyond the settlement. Since he was almost totally blind without them it took him until noon the next day to find his way back to Muddy Hole. That whole day was a total loss to us. Without his glasses Enos could not work, and without Enos, Obie would not work.

The situation was saved when Jack hired the entire juvenile population to go on a spectacle hunt. He persuaded the schoolteacher, a pale young man who did not like teaching anyway, to declare a holiday and he offered a prize of one dollar in silver coins to the person who found Enos's glasses.

The youngsters went at the job with marvellous enthusiasm. They scoured the countryside for miles around and eventually, and against all odds, they found the missing spectacles.

They were hanging from the branch of a spruce tree, some ten feet above the ground. To this day, nobody has any sure knowledge of how they got there. The story that they were tossed into the tree by an irate caribou cannot be substantiated, but neither can it be categorically rejected.

7. *Full speed astern*

AFTER SPENDING a single night under Enos's roof, Jack insisted we shift aboard the boat. He was reluctant to give reasons but the presence of seven nubile young women seemed to unnerve him. His back was still a dubious quantity. In any event, we took up housekeeping aboard our own little vessel.

When I originally gave Enos instructions for converting the boat into a cruising yacht he appeared to understand me well enough, but when he began doing the work my wishes came into conflict with centuries of tradition – tradition which dictated that the space occupied by people on any vessel must be reduced to the irreducible minimum, leaving as much room as possible for fish, engines, and other really vital things. Tradition also dictated that the accommodations must be as uncomfortable as possible, presumably to ensure that the crew had small alternative to remaining on deck working their fishing gear, even in the midst of a winter gale.

Enos's attempts to carry out my instructions, in opposition to his own deep-rooted instincts, led to a compromise that was no happy one. He began by building the immense cabin trunk, which I have already referred to as looking like an upside-down coffin, over the fish wells; but although he made it as high as a barn on the sides, he did not camber the

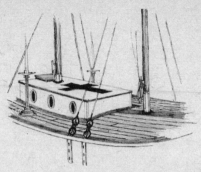

roof, with the result that there was only five feet of head-room down below. It was necessary to walk about in the cabin with one's knees well bent or else with one's head laid over upon a shoulder. Tall men could not walk at all. They had to crawl.

The cabin was of ample length but Enos had found a way to fix that too. He partitioned off the after-third to house the great green monster that was our engine. There was no doubt about it – the engine had the best accommodation on the ship.

In what small space remained Enos roughed in the accom-modation for human beings, and the verb is fully descriptive. He built two bunks right up in the eyes of the vessel, hard against the chain locker, and he built them to traditional specifications: sixteen inches wide at the head, twelve inches wide at the foot, and sixty-six inches long. He somehow also managed to tip the bunks so that the occupant's feet were six inches higher than his head. As a final touch, he made the side-boards (which are intended to keep you in place when the vessel grows lively) out of unplaned black spruce, than which there is no more splintery material known to man.

All in all, the design was diabolically efficient, for it guar-anteed that any man who could stay in those bunks longer than twenty minutes at a time had to be close to dissolution.

In Enos's view, living space on a fishing vessel ought to consist only of a place to sleep and a place to cook. He there-fore turned the small remaining space in the cabin into a galley. He provided a place for a stove, and enough lockers wherein to stow hardtack, salt pork, flour, and turnips for at least forty men on a voyage to Tierra del Fuego and back again – non-stop.

Lockers (cupboards to landlubbers) were the one thing the cabin did not lack. In days to come, members of the crew who had suffered as much mortification in the bunks as the flesh could endure sometimes crawled into the lockers, shoving aside their contents, in order to get a little rest.

When I first saw what Enos had done I ordered him to tear everything out and start again. This soured him and a sour Enos was an intractable Enos. He told me it would take not less than two months to change things around and so, perforce, I had to let the matter drop. However I did prevail upon him to add a saloon table. Although it was very small it pre-empted most of the remaining floor space.

This was the home Jack and I moved into. It was not yet painted. It was filled with oddments of gear, pieces of wood, coils of rope, and a stench that drew its potency equally from the bilges and from the fish-plant soup in which we floated. Home was unprepossessing but it was at least free of ebullient and uninhibited women – and it was very conveniently located in relation to Enos's fish store.

During the first ten days we lived aboard we did not suffer much discomfort from the bunks because we seldom had a chance to use them. We worked by day, and we worked by night. We ate when there was nothing better to do and though I consider myself a competent cook my culinary productions were not up to much during this period.

I cooked on a gasoline stove and the staple food was cod. This was not a matter of choice. It resulted from a desperate attempt on our part to prevent the ship from reverting to her original role and filling up to the hatches with codfish. The fishermen in Muddy Hole were, one and all, hospitable and generous men. Every morning when they returned from hauling their cod traps each of the boats would come alongside and her skipper would present us with a fine, fat cod for dinner.

Because the harbour was the most public place in Muddy

Hole and our boat was almost never free of visitors, we could not dispose of the surplus fish over the side. Had it been reported that we had thrown away one single fish, every inhabitant in the settlement would have been hurt to the quick, and we would have become virtual pariahs.

So we ate cod in unbelievable quantities. We ate it boiled, fried, poached, and once, when Jack undertook to cook dinner, raw. Nevertheless, we could not begin to keep up with the supply until Obie took pity on us and converted our surplus into salt-pickled cod which we stored in a huge barrel in his store.

By the last week in July the vessel was beginning to look vaguely shipshape. She was rigged with gear that was heavy enough to meet the needs of a vessel three times her size. Her sails, cut from fourteen-gauge canvas, were bent; and I may say they were not easy to bend, since they were made of a material with the stiffness and weight of galvanized iron. The propeller had been shipped during a hideous episode which saw Jack and Enos and me wading knee deep in slime throughout most of one interminable day. The bare places on her upperworks and decks had received at least one coat of paint – variegated paint, because we had to use the odds and ends we could find at the bottom of paint cans scrounged from fishermen's stores. Water and gas tanks had been installed and the water tank had been filled by Jack. The source of water was a spring half a mile away on the hillside which dripped a quart of water an hour. It took Jack two days to fill the tank.

Most of the essential equipment was aboard and had found a place in which to live, at least temporarily. There remained only one area of real uncertainty – the engine. Since she looms all too large in what follows I shall give a detailed introduction to her. She was a seven-horsepower, single-cylinder, make-and-break, gasoline-fuelled monster, built in the 1920's from an original design conceived somewhere near the end of

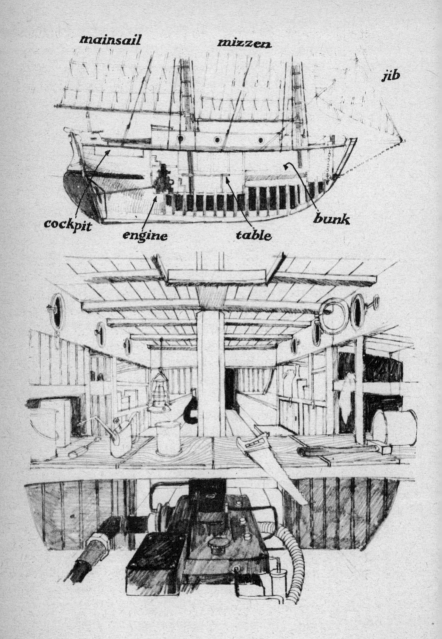

the last century. She was massive beyond belief, and intractable beyond bearing. In order to start her it was first necessary to open a priming cock on the cylinder head and introduce half a cup of raw gasoline. Then you had to spin her flywheel which was as big as the wheel of a freight car and weighed about the same.

There was no clutch and no gear box. When, and if, the engine started, the boat immediately began to move. She did not necessarily move forward. It is an idiosyncrasy of the make-and-breaks that when they start they may choose to turn over either to left or to right (which is to say either forward or astern), and there is no way known to man of predicting which direction it is going to be.

Once started, the direction can be reversed only by snatching off the spark-wire and letting the engine almost die. On its next-to-final kick it will usually backfire and in the process reverse itself, at which instant one must push the spark-wire back in place and hope that the beast will continue turning over. It seldom does. At least it seldom did for Jack and me. To properly dominate a make-and-break engine one must have grown up with it from childhood.

According to mythology the virtue of these engines lies in the fact that they are simple and reliable. Although this myth is widely believed I am able to report that it is completely untrue. These engines are, in fact, vindictive, debased, black-minded ladies of no virtue and any non-Newfoundlander who goes shipmates with one is either a fool or a masochist, and is likely both.

We ran our first engine test on a Sunday morning and, for a wonder, the sun was shining in Muddy Hole and the fog had retreated out to sea. It was therefore an auspicious morning, but the auspices proved misleading. Enos and Obie were on hand to demonstrate the engine to us, but although both of them had lived with make-and-breaks all their lives it took them an hour to get the beast going. When she did start it was with a bellowing roar that reminded us we had been unable to find a muffler for her. She started in reverse, but this was of no moment since we had moored the schooner to the stage with enough lines to hold the *Queen Mary*. The big blade turned and stirred up the bottom muck, so that great gaseous bubbles began to burst under her counter, testifying to unknown horrors of corruption in the depths below.

Jack and I did not observe much of this first-hand. We were too busy leaping for our lives. The moment she started, the green monster went berserk. With each stroke of her huge piston she leapt a good four inches off the wooden bedding plates, and then came down again with a jolt that shook our little ship from keel to masthead. At each jolt, the open-topped carburetor flung a spray of gasoline over the battery box and over the hot exhaust pipe.

Since it seemed obvious that the vessel was going to explode Jack and I flung ourselves on deck, gained the stage head and ran for our lives. We did not halt until we were safely behind the shelter of Enos's house. However when a few minutes later the bellow of the engine ceased and there had been no colossal bang, we cautiously returned to the harbour. We found Enos and Obie unconcernedly awaiting us. They explained what had taken place.

When he originally built the boat Enos bedded the engine with iron bolts and during her years with the Hallohans these had rusted out. The Hallohans had not attempted to replace them, but had devised a system of two-by-four wooden shores, which they had braced all over the engine room and which served to hold the monster in its place. During the refit Enos removed these shores without stopping to consider what, if any, purpose they served. He now knew, as did we all.

Replacing the bolts was a tedious task. The vessel had to be dried out again at low tide and holes drilled right through her bottom, into which we fitted big bronze keeper bolts taken from the boiler of a wrecked coasting steamer. Enos was of the opinion that *these* would hold, and in this instance he was right.

When next we ran the bullgine (this is the nicest of the names we devised for her), she stayed put in her place, and that was a blessing, although it did not solve all our problems. Foremost of these was the fact that neither Jack nor I could get her to start. We did not have the knack, neither did we have the muscle. Since I had become the self-appointed skipper of the vessel I used my prerogatives to appoint Jack to the position of chief engineer and turned my mind to other things.

I must pay him homage. Throughout most of one day he wrestled with the beast under the tutelage of Obie. Toward evening, exhausted and filthy, wordless with fury but still indomitable, he finally got her to go. She immediately backfired, kicked into reverse all on her own, spun the flywheel the wrong way around, and caught Jack on the elbow with the starting handle, propelling him full length into the main cabin.

His was something of a Pyrrhic victory since his back went out and his elbow swelled up so he could not even feed himself properly, let alone raise a glass with his right hand. Furthermore it was a victory in a single battle only and on every subsequent occasion when he had to start the engine the victory had to be won anew.

The Hallohans' failure to name the boat was their own business. We had no intention of girdling the world in a nameless ship. Off and on we thought about the matter and we almost decided she should be called *Black Joke.*

The original *Black Joke* was a particularly infamous slaver sailing between West Africa and Virginia. She made a desperate reputation for herself. Her accommodation was so bad that a large part of her hapless passengers died of it. She also had the reputation of carrying such a stink that her presence could be detected aboard ships fifty miles to leeward of her. In general, the name seemed apt even if our vessel was green instead of black.

One night Jack and I visited the Morrys to cleanse ourselves physically and spiritually, and Howard began yarning

about Peter Easton, gentleman and captain in the Royal Navy who, early in the seventeenth century, decided to better himself by going into business on his own. He became one of the most successful pirates of all time. With a fleet that at one time numbered thirty vessels he dominated the sea routes between Europe and North America. He captured the Governor of Newfoundland and virtually made that island his personal domain.

Using it as a base, he raided the Caribbean, even capturing Morro Castle, together with its governor. On another foray far afield he captured four vessels of the Spanish treasure squadron off the Azores and took them to Tunis. The Bey of Tunis promptly concluded an *equal* alliance with Peter who then set out to singe the beard of the King of Spain. He did this so effectively that the royal Spanish fleet refused to face him in open battle and remained bottled up in its home harbours for more than a year. By this time Peter was growing weary of the active life, so he blackmailed the King of England into granting him a pardon, after which he retired to the Duchy of Savoy, bought himself a vast estate and the rank of Marquis, and gave up the sea.

Peter Easton was unique. He never made anyone walk the plank. He paid his men well and treated them decently. He had a sharp sense of humour. He was kind and loving – very loving, it is said – to women.

Jack fell completely under the Easton spell, possibly because of a psychological phenomenon known as transfer identification. He became such an Easton fan that he insisted we call our ship after Peter's flag ship – the ironically named *Happy Adventure*.

I at first demurred, being well aware that it would be necessary in future to offer long explanations for such a choice to critics who thought the name was simply too sentimental to be true. However in the end Jack won.

We did not have a traditional christening ceremony since nobody in Muddy Hole would have tolerated the waste of a bottle of anything alcoholic. Instead we sat in her crowded cabin one evening and drank a number of toasts to the rein-carnation of Peter Easton's ship. Then we pumped *Happy Adventure* dry (it now took only an hour or so) and bade our guests goodnight. We had determined to try our wings upon the morrow.

Seamen refer to the first tentative voyage of a newly com-missioned ship as her trials. *Happy Adventure*'s trials began at 1400 hours the next day, and so did ours.

It was a "civil" day (in Newfoundland this means the wind is not blowing a full hurricane) and a stiff easterly was whitening the waters of the harbour. Because this was our first departure, and because we were being watched by most of the inhabitants of Muddy Hole, we felt compelled to leave the stage under full sail.

We did not do too badly. With main, foresail, jib, and jumbo hoisted, Jack cast off our moorings. We sheeted every-thing home, the heavy sails began to draw and *Happy Adventure* slowly picked up way. In a few moments she was standing swiftly across the harbour.

In order to get out of the long narrow harbour of Muddy Hole against an east wind a vessel under sail must beat to weather – that is, she must tack back and forth against the wind. We were, of course, aware of this necessity. We were also aware that, as we left the stage, directly ahead of us there lay a covey of two dozen dories and skiffs, moored fifty yards off shore. As we approached them I prepared to come about on the other tack.

"Ready about!" I sang out to Jack. Then, pushing the big tiller over, "Hard a'lee!"

Happy Adventure's head came up into the wind. She shook herself a bit, considered whether she would come about or not – and decided not. Her head fell off again and she resumed her original course.

Jack was later to claim that this was one of the few honest things she ever did. He claimed she knew perfectly well what would happen if we ever took her to sea, and so she decided it would be better for all of us if she committed suicide immediately by skewering herself on the rocky shores of her home port, where her bones could rest in peace forever.

I disagree. I think that, never having been under sail before, the poor little vessel simply did not know what was expected of her. I think she was as terrified as I was as she bore down on the defenceless mess of little boats and the rocks that lay beyond them.

It was Jack who saved us all. He did not even pause to curse, but leapt into the engine room with such alacrity that he caught the bullgine sleeping. Before it knew he was there he had spun the flywheel and, even without a prime, the green beast was so surprised she fired. She had been taken totally off guard, but even as she belched into life she struck back at us, thinking to make us pay for our trickery by starting in reverse.

There were a great many people watching from the fish-plant wharf. Since they could not hear the roar of the bullgine above the thunder of the plant machinery they were incredulous of what they saw. Under full sail and snoring bravely along, *Happy Adventure* slowly came to a stop. Then with all sails still set and drawing—she began to back up. The fish-plant manager, a worldly man who had several times seen motion picture films, said it was like watching a movie that had been reversed. He said he expected to see the schooner back right up Obie's stage, lower her sails, and go to sleep again.

I would have been happy to have had this happen. To tell the truth I was so unnerved that it was on the tip of my tongue to turn command over to Jack, jump into our little dory which we were towing astern, and abandon the sea forever. However pride is a terrible taskmaster and I dared not give in to my better instincts.

It was now obvious to Jack and to me that we were not going to be able to beat out of the harbour and that we would have to go out under power if we were to get out at all. But neither of us cared to try to make the bullgine change direction and drive the boat ahead. We knew perfectly well she would stop, and refuse to start, and leave us to drift ignominiously ashore. Consequently, *Happy Adventure backed* all the way out of Muddy Hole harbour under full sail. I think it must have been the most reluctant departure in the history of men and ships.

Once we were at sea, and safely clear of the great headlands guarding the harbour mouth, Jack did try to reverse the engine and she reacted as we had known she would. She stopped and would not start. It no longer mattered. *Happy Adventure* lay over on her bilge, took the wind over her port bow and went bowling off down the towering coast as if she was on her way to a racing rendezvous.

During the next few hours all the miseries, doubts, and distresses of the past weeks vanished from our minds. The little ship sailed like a good witch. She still refused to come about, but this was no great problem in open water since we could jibe her around, and her masts and rigging were so stout that this sometimes dangerous practice threatened her not at all. We sailed her on a broad reach; we sailed her hard on the wind; we let her run, hung-out, with foresail to starboard and mainsail to port; and we had no fault to find with her seakeeping qualities.

She had, however, some other frailties. The unaccustomed motion of bucketing through big seas under a press of canvas squeezed out most of the fish gunk with which she had sealed her seams, and she began to leak so excessively that Jack had to spend most of his time at the pump. Also, the massive compass I had brought with me from Ontario demonstrated an incredible disdain for convention, and insisted on pointing as much as forty degrees off what should have been the correct course. It was apparent that, until we found someone who could adjust the compass, our navigation would have to be, in the time-honoured phrase, "by guess and by God." Neither of us was a very good guesser and we did not know how much we could rely on God.

In our temporarily euphoric mood we dared to sail several miles off shore to reconnoitre a belated iceberg. We were circling it at a discreet distance, for the great bergs become unstable in late summer and sometimes turn turtle, setting up tidal waves that can swamp a small vessel, when the sun began to haze over. The Grand Banks fog was rolling in upon the back of the east wind.

We fled before it and *Happy Adventure* carried us swiftly between the headlands of the harbour just as the fog overtook us, providing a grey escort as we ran down the reach and rounded-to in fine style at Obie's stage.

Despite her unorthodox departure, and despite the leaks and the compass, we felt reasonably content with our little vessel and not a little proud of ourselves as well. We were as ready as we would ever be to begin our voyage.

8· *The Old Man earns his drink*

ONE SMALL difficulty still remained. We had no charts of the east coast of Newfoundland. The lack of charts, combined with a misleading compass and the dead certainty of running into fog, suggested we would do well to ship a pilot until we could make a port where charts could be bought and the compass adjusted.

The obvious choice for a pilot was Enos. Like most Newfoundland seamen he possessed, we presumed, special senses which are lost to modern man. He had sailed these waters all his life, often without a compass and usually without charts. When you asked him how he managed to find his way to some distant place he would look baffled and reply:

"Well, me son, I *knows* where it's at."

We needed somebody like that. However when we broached the matter to Enos he showed no enthusiasm. For a man who was usually as garrulous as an entire pack of politicians, his response was spectacularly succinct.

"No!" he grunted, and for emphasis spat a gob of tobacco juice on our newly painted cabin top.

There was no swaying him either. Persuasion (and Jack is a persuader *par excellence*) got us nowhere. He kept on saying "No" and spitting until the cabin top developed a slippery brown sheen over most of its surface and we were prepared to give up. I was, at any rate, but Jack was made of sterner stuff.

"If the old bustard won't come willingly," Jack told me after Enos left, "we'll shanghai him."

"The hell with him, Jack. Forget it. We'll manage on our own."

"Forget him nothing! If this goddamn boat sinks I'm at least going to have the satisfaction of seeing him sink with it!"

There was no arguing with Jack in a mood like that.

He arranged a small farewell party on board that night. It was one of the gloomiest parties I have ever attended. Six or seven of our fishermen friends squeezed into the cabin and ruminated at lugubrious length on the manifold perils of the sea. When they got tired of that, they began recalling the small schooners that had sailed out of Southern Shore ports and never been heard of again. The list went on and on until even Enos began to grow restive.

"Well, byes," he interjected, "them was mostly poor-built boats. Not fitten to go to sea. Not proper fer it, ye might say. Now you takes a boat like this 'un. Proper built and found. *She* won't be making ary widows on the shore."

This was the opening Jack had been waiting for.

"You're so right, Enos. In a boat as good as this a fellow could sail to hell and back."

Enos eyed Jack with sudden suspicion. "Aye," he replied cautiously. "She be good fer it!"

"*You* certainly wouldn't be afraid to sail in her, now would you Enos?"

The trap was sprung.

"Well, now, me darlin' man, I don't say as I wouldn't, but a'course . . . ."

"Good enough!" Jack shouted. "Farley, hand me the log. Enos, we'll sign you on as sailing master for the maiden voyage of the finest ship you ever built."

Enos struggled mightily but to no avail. He was under the eyes of six of his peers and one of them, without realizing it, became our ally:

"Sign on, sign on, Enos, me son. We knows you'm not afeard!"

So Enos signed his mark.

Happy Adventure sailed an hour after dawn. It was a fine morning, clear and warm, with a good draft of wind out of the nor'west to help us on our way and to keep the fog off shore. We had intended to sail *at* dawn but Enos did not turn up and when we went to look for him his daughters said he had gone off to haul a herring net. We recognized this as a ruse, and so we searched for him in the most likely place. He was savagely disgruntled when we found him, complaining bitterly that a man couldn't even "do his nature" without being followed. Little by little we coaxed him down to the stage, got him aboard and down below, and before he could rally, we cast off the lines.

Happy Adventure made a brave sight as she rolled down the reach toward the waiting sea. With all sails set and drawing she lay over a little and snored sweetly through the water actually overtaking and passing two or three belated trap skiffs bound out to the fishing grounds. Their crews grinned cheerfully at us, which is as close to a farewell as a Newfoundland seaman will allow himself. There is bad luck in farewells.

Before we cleared the headlands I celebrated a small ritual that I learned from my father. I poured four stiff glasses of rum. I gave one of these to Enos and one to Jack, and I kept one for myself. The fourth, I poured overboard. The Old Man of the Sea is a sailor and he likes his drop of grog. And it is a good thing to be on friendly terms with the Old Man when you venture out upon the grey waters that are his domain.

All that morning we sailed south on a long reach keeping a two- or three-mile offing from the grim sea cliffs. We came abeam of Cape Ballard and left it behind, then the wind began to fall light and fickle, ghosting for a change. The change came and the wind picked up from sou'east, a dead muzzler right on our bows, bringing the fog in toward us.

Enos began to grow agitated. We were approaching Cape Race, the southeast "corner" of Newfoundland and one of the most feared places in the Western Ocean. Its peculiar menace lies in the tidal currents that sweep past it. They are totally unpredictable. They can carry an unwary vessel, or one blinded by fog, miles off her true course and so to destruction on the brooding rocks ashore.

In our innocence Jack and I were not much worried and when Enos insisted that we down sail and start the engine we were inclined to mock him. He did not like this and withdrew into sullen taciturnity, made worse by the fact that I had closed off the rum rations while we were at sea. Finally, to please him, we started the bullgine, or rather Jack did, after a blasphemous half hour's struggle.

The joys of the day were now all behind us. Sombre clouds began closing off the sky; the air grew chill, presaging the coming of the fog; and the thunderous blatting of the unmuffled bullgine deafened us, while the slow strokes of the great piston shook the little boat as an otter shakes a trout.

By four o'clock we still had reasonably good visibility and were abeam of Cape Race—and there we stuck. The engine thundered and the water boiled under our counter but we got no farther on our way. Hour after hour the massive highlands behind the cape refused to slip astern. Jack and I finally began to comprehend something of the power of the currents. Although we were making five knots through the water a lee bow tide was running at almost the same speed against us.

86

The fog was slow in coming but the wall of grey slid inexorably nearer. At six-thirty Jack went below to rustle up some food. An instant later his head appeared in the companionway. The air of casual insouciance, which was as much a part of his seagoing gear as his jaunty yachting cap, had vanished.

"Christ!" he cried, and it was perhaps partly a prayer. "This bloody boat is sinking!"

I jumped to join him and found that he was undeniably right. Water was already sluicing across the floor boards in the main cabin. Spread-eagling the engine for better purchase, Jack began working the handle of the pump as if his life depended on it. It dawned on me his life *did* depend on it; and so did mine.

The next thing I knew Enos had shouldered me aside. Taking one horrified look at the private swimming pool inside *Happy Adventure*, he shrieked:

"Lard Jasus, byes, she's gone!"

It was hardly the remark we needed to restore our faith in him or in his boat. Still yelling, he went on to diagnose the trouble.

He told us the stuffing box had fallen off. This meant that the ocean was free to enter the boat through the large hole in the sternpost that housed the vessel's shaft. And since we could not reach it there was nothing we could do about it.

Enos now retreated into a mental room of his own, a dark hole filled with fatalistic thoughts. However, by giving him a bottle of rum to cherish, I managed to persuade him to take the tiller (the little boat had meanwhile been going in circles) and steer a course for Trepassey Bay, fifteen miles to the eastward, where I thought we might just manage to beach the vessel before she sank.

There was never any question of abandoning her. Our dory, so called, was a little plywood box barely capable of carrying one man. Life-preservers would have been useless, because we were in the Labrador Current where the waters are so cold that a man cannot survive immersion in them for

more than a few minutes.

By dint of furious pumping, Jack and I found we could almost hold the water level where it was, although we could not gain upon the inflow. And so we pumped. The engine thundered on. We pumped. The minutes stretched into hours and we pumped. The fog held off, which was one minor blessing, and we pumped. The engine roared and the heat became so intense that we were sweating almost as much water back into the bilges as we were pumping out. We pumped. The tidal current slackened and turned and began to help us on our way. We pumped.

Occasionally one of us crawled on deck to breathe and to rest our agonized muscles for a moment. At eight o'clock I stuck my head out of the companionway and saw the massive headland of Mistaken Point a mile or so to leeward. I glanced at Enos. He was staring straight ahead, his eyes half shut and his mouth pursed into a dark pit of despair. He had taken out his dentures, a thing he always did in moments of stress. When I called out to tell him we were nearly holding the leak he gave no sign of hearing but continued staring over the bow as if he beheld some bleak and terrible vision from which he could not take his attention for a moment. Not at all cheered I ducked back into the engine room.

And then the main pump jammed.

That pump was a fool of a thing that had no right to be aboard a boat. Its innards were a complicated mass of springs and valves that could not possibly digest the bits of flotsam, jetsam, and codfish floating in the vessel's bilge. But, fool of a thing or not, it was our only hope.

It was dark by this time so Jack held a flashlight while I unbolted the pump's face plate. The thing contained ten small coil springs and all of them leapt for freedom the instant the plate came off. They ricocheted off the cabin sides like a swarm of manic bees and fell, to sink below the surface of the water in the bilges.

It does not seem possible, but we found them all. It took twenty-five or thirty minutes of groping with numbed arms under oily, icy water, but we found them all, re-installed them, put back the face plate, and again began to pump.

Meanwhile the water had gained four inches. It was now over the lower part of the flywheel and less than two inches below the top of the carburetor. The flywheel spun a niagara of spray onto the red-hot exhaust pipe, turning the dark and roaring engine-room into a sauna bath. We pumped.

Jack crawled on deck for a breather and immediately gave a frantic yell. For a second I hesitated. I did not think I had the fortitude to face a new calamity—but a second urgent summons brought me out on deck. Enos was frozen at the helm and by the last light of day I could see he was steering straight toward a wall of rock which loomed above us, no more than three hundred yards away.

I leapt for the tiller. Enos did not struggle but meekly moved aside. His expression had changed and had become almost beatific. It may have been the rum that did it – Enos was at peace with himself and with the Fates.

"We'd best run her onto the rocks," he explained mildly, "than be drowned in the cold, cold water."

Jack went back to the pump and I put the vessel on a course to skirt the threatening cliffs. We were not impossibly far from Trepassey Bay, and there still seemed to be a chance we could reach the harbour and beach the vessel on a non-lethal shore.

At about eleven o'clock I saw a flashing light ahead and steered for it. When I prodded him Enos confirmed that it might be the buoy marking the entrance to Trepassey harbour. However before we reached it the fog overtook us and the darkness became total. We felt our way past the light-buoy and across the surrounding shoals with only luck and the Old Man to guide us.

As we entered the black gut which we hoped was the harbour entrance, I did not need Jack's warning shout to tell me that our time had about run out. The bullgine had begun to cough and splutter. The water level had reached her carburetor and, tough as she was, she could not remain alive for long on a mixture of gasoline and salt sea water.

Within Trepassey harbour all was inky black. No lights could be seen on the invisible shore. I steered blindly ahead, knowing that sooner or later we must strike the land. Then the engine coughed, stopped, picked up again, coughed, and stopped for good. Silently, in that black night, the little ship ghosted forward.

Jack came tumbling out on deck for there was no point in remaining below while the vessel foundered. He had, and I remember this with great clarity, a flashlight in his mouth and a bottle of rum in each hand . . . .

. . . At that moment *Happy Adventure*'s forefoot hit something. She jarred a little, made a strange sucking sound, and the motion went out of her.

"I t'inks," said Enos as he nimbly relieved Jack of one of the bottles, "I t'inks we's runned ashore!"

Jack believes *Happy Adventure* has a special kind of homing instinct. He may be right. Certainly she is never happier than when she is lying snuggled up against a working fish-plant. Perhaps she identifies fish plants with the natal womb, which is not so strange when one remembers she was built in a fish-plant yard and that she spent the many months of her refit as a semi-permanent fixture in the fish-plant slip at Muddy Hole.

In any event when she limped into Trepassey she unerringly found her way straight to her spiritual home. Even before we began playing flashlights on our surroundings we knew this was so. The old familiar stench rose all around us like a dank miasma.

The flashlights revealed that we had run ashore on a gently shelving beach immediately alongside a massively constructed wharf. Further investigation had to be delayed because the tide was falling and the schooner was in danger of keeling over on her bilge. Jack made a jump and managed to scale the face of the wharf. He caught the lines I threw him and we rigged a spider web of ropes from our two masts to the wharf timbers to hold the vessel upright when all the water had drained away from under her.

When she seemed secure I joined Jack on the dock and cautiously we went exploring. The fog was so thick that our lights were nearly useless and we practically bumped into the first human being we encountered. He was the night watchman for Industrial Seafood Packers, a huge concern to whose dock we were moored. After we had convinced the watchman that we did not have a cargo of fish to unload, but were only mariners in distress, he came aboard.

He seemed genuinely incredulous to find we did not have a radar set. How, he asked, had we found our way into the harbour? How had we missed striking the several draggers anchored in the fairway? And how, in hell's own name (his words), had we found the plant and managed to come alongside the wharf without hitting the L-shaped end where the cod-oil factory stood in lonely grandeur?

Since we could not answer these questions we evaded them, leaving him with the suspicion, which spread rapidly around Trepassey, that we were possessed by an occult power. Witches and warlocks have not yet vanished from the outport scene in Newfoundland.

The watchman was a generous man and he told us we could stay at the wharf as long as we wished. He felt, however, that we might be happier if we moored a hundred feet farther to seaward.

" 'Tis the poipe, ye know; the poipe what carries off the gurry from the plant. Ye've moored hard alongside o' she."

Happy Adventure had come home with a vengeance and, for all I know, it may have *been* vengeance at that.

That was a singularly dreadful night.

We had to begin repairing the leak immediately, while the tide was low. We soon found that Enos's diagnosis had been correct. The outside stuffing box, or gland, had come adrift when both retaining lag screws parted, allowing the box to slip down the shaft until it rested against the propeller.

In order to repair it we had to borrow a big drill from the helpful watchman, drill out the remains of the old lag screws, fair off the dead wood where the shaft had chewed it up, and then screw the gland back into place. Perhaps this does not sound like much of a task, but let me try to paint the scene.

To reach the gland we had to wade knee-deep in black, stinking muck, a composite product consisting of aboriginal slime fortified over the decades by decaying contributions from the fish plant. We worked in darkness except for the light from two poor flashlights which could produce only a dim orange glow in the shroud of bitterly cold fog that enveloped us. We kept dropping things, and the recovery of a wrench or a bolt from the sucking slime brought to mind Hercules at his task in the Augean stables.

By three o'clock the job was done and just in time because

the tide was rising. We waited impatiently for it to float the boat so we could haul her out along the wharf, away from the ominous presence of the "poipe." Half an hour before the plant began operations, the tide was full.

It was not full enough. *Happy Adventure* did not float.

We had run her ashore "on the last of springs," which is to say, on the highest tide of the month. Enos, who knew all about such things, pointed out to us it would be nearly twenty-eight days before the tide was as high again.

Enos also said he felt it was time for him to leave. He said he did not want to be a bother to us and, considering the cramped accommodation on our little vessel and the fact that we would be making a prolonged visit in Trepassey, he thought it would be better if he went away as soon as the fog thinned. He said he would sacrifice his own comfort and stay with friends ashore until he could find transportation back to Muddy Hole.

I did not attempt to dissuade him but Jack was displeased because, as an old Navy man, he took a dim view of people jumping ship. However after breakfast Jack found he was able to accept Enos's departure with equanimity.

I cooked that breakfast. It was a hearty one for we were all half-starved. I cut up and fried about three pounds of side bacon. It was fat bacon; it was tough bacon; and it had a rind on it a quarter of an inch thick.

Jack and Enos sat at the saloon table while I served them. What with the layers of muck that coated our clothing, and what with the stench from the fishy flats outside, the atmosphere was not salubrious. However for once Jack was too tired, too hungry, and too depressed to care about his mealtime surroundings. Grimly he went to work on his bacon while I turned back to the stove to cook my own rashers. Suddenly I heard Jack make a despairing, strangled sound. I spun around.

Jack sat rigid on the bench, his eyes staring glassily from a face that had lost its usual ruddy colour and had become grotesquely mottled. He was staring at Enos.

All unaware of the scrutiny Enos was busy eating his bacon. It had proved too tough for him to deal with while his badly fitting dentures remained in his mouth, so he had removed both plates. He now held them firmly in the angle between thumb and forefinger of his left hand, and he was making them snap open and shut with a dexterity that argued long practice. With his right hand he was passing a strip of bacon between the two sets of grinders. When this remarkable operation had macerated the strip of bacon sufficiently he threw back his head, poised the bacon over his mouth, and gummed it down.

Jack struggled to his feet, pushed his way past me, and vanished out the companion hatch. Before he returned, an hour or so later, Enos had packed his gear and gone ashore. I cannot in all conscience say that either of us was deeply pained to sign him off.

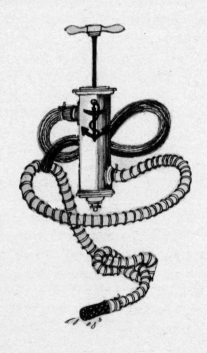

9· *T'place where t'fog is made*

Trepassey clings forlornly to the southeastern tip of Newfoundland. It is a windswept, desolate little village whose grey wooden houses straggle dismally around the edge of a broad harbour. Behind them the treeless hills roll upward to the interior barrens of the Avalon Peninsula. However these bleak surroundings are seldom seen. Trepassey is, as they say in other parts of Newfoundland, "t'place where t'fog is made."

I believe it. *Happy Adventure* lay in Trepassey for almost a week, and during that time we never knew if the sun still shone somewhere, or if it had been extinguished by some cosmic cataclysm. We lived in a world of shadows and uncertain outlines where nothing seemed quite real – nothing, that is, except the fish plant. *It* was indubitably real.

It was a busier plant than its sister at Muddy Hole. Despite its drab and gloomy character, Trepassey has been a haven for Grand Banks fishermen through more than four hundred years. It too has known the fishing fleets of the early Basques, of Spaniards, of Portuguese, of the French, and finally of the English. It was still very busy when we were there. All day long and far into each night the muffled thump of engines from unseen vessels in the fog told us of the comings and goings of a motley fleet of long-liners, draggers, and small craft, which had gathered here from outports hundreds of miles away to take their share of the summer run of cod.

Nothing about our stay at Trepassey provides memories upon which I care to dwell, but the day of Enos's departure was so horrible that even my notes written at the time fail to deal adequately with it.

Enos departs at 7 A.M., the last I hear of him is a grand final expectoration on deck. I hope it is only tobacco juice and spit, not bacon. Jack can't stand much more. . . . At 8 A.M. the sewage tank at the plant got up its first full head of steam and let her rip. The discharge shot ten feet out of the pipe and did not quite clear H.A.'s deck. Most of it hit the mainmast and was deflected into the cockpit. Discharge continues about once every hour. Like Big Bertha at the siege of Paris, but Paris never could have stood up to this barrage . . . . Out of rum. Last bottle seems to have disappeared . . . . Tide fell and rose again, one foot short of refloating us . . . . Jack offered to sell H.A. "as is, where is," to local fisherman for fifty dollars. Was refused. . . . Manager fish plant came along at noon, asked us to move. Said we are interfering with flow from sewage pipe. Jack made highly personal suggestion to manager where he could put sewer pipe. Was refused . . . . Discover no rum available closer than St. John's. Jack beginning to talk longingly of life of book publisher in Toronto . . . . Small boy aboard at 4:30 offers Jack a rusty tin can full of cod's tongues for ten cents. Was refused . . . . Stink in cabin so atrocious Jack opened portlight over his bunk, forgetting next discharge from pipe was due. Failed to get portlight closed in time . . . .

It was a hideous day but the climax came that evening. Just after supper, for which neither of us had any stomach, Jack decided to light the gasoline lantern. This lantern was a piece of equipment we seldom used, preferring to depend on the dim light from two small oil lamps which, we felt, were less likely to ignite the ever-present raw gasoline floating in our bilge. However this night we needed the big lantern, not only because its garish flare might brighten the general gloom, but also because it would provide much-needed heat which, to some small extent, might dispel the stinking damp that filled the cabin, and that had turned our sleeping-bags and clothing into clammy corpse shrouds.

For safety's sake Jack normally took the lantern on deck or ashore before lighting it, but this evening he was not normal. He may even, although he denies it, have had some hope in his subconscious mind that the thing *would* explode and put us out of our misery. Whatever the case, he chose to light it on the saloon table, and when he opened the valve to prime the generator, he opened it too far and left it open too long. When he touched a match to the mantle a three-foot flame leapt into instant life.

Whatever desire for self-immolation may have lurked in the back of Jack's mind, it was no match for his instinct for self-preservation. Thrusting a long wooden spoon (with which I had mixed our codfish stew) under the lantern's handle, he leapt for the companionway, scrambled through it, and disappeared into the night waving his flaming torch and shouting, "Fire!" at the top of his lungs.

There were a great many boats and vessels moored to the wharf that night, including three big, new side-draggers that boasted all sorts of modern equipment, including Foamite fire-control systems. Acting on the assumption that it would be quicker to take the fire to the extinguisher than to wait for the extinguisher to come to him, Jack made straight for these draggers. His path took him between several rows of forty-five gallon drums, painted red, and filled with gasoline for the use of the smaller fishing boats. His urgent bellowing and the great flare of light that accompanied him alerted all the crews of the moored boats, and by the time he neared the draggers he had a large, attentive, and terrified audience.

What the final outcome *might* have been is anybody's guess. I like to dwell on the possibility that Jack might have succeeded in boarding one of the draggers bearing his burning offering and there been received with such a blizzard of CO_2 foam that he would have been buried alive.

The reality was not quite so dramatic. Before reaching the first dragger Jack discovered that the wooden spoon had caught fire and was burning briskly. He knew he was not going to make it. Reacting with the split-second reflexes for which he is justly famed, he swerved to the dockside and flung spoon and lantern into the cold sea. There was a brief final flare as the last of the gasoline burned on the surface before darkness closed down upon us all.

By the time Jack fumbled his way back to *Happy Adventure* (he had been half-blinded by the glare), I had lit the cabin lamps. We said nothing to each other; we just sat in silence until, half an hour later, heavy boots clumped on our deck and a gruff voice asked permission to come below.

Permission being granted four very large, very muscular, fishing skippers crammed their way into the cabin.

They said they had heard we were having trouble refloating our boat. They said they would deem it an honour (those were not exactly the words they used) to give us a helping hand. They said their crews were already rigging wire warps from our bows to the main winch of the biggest dragger. Would we, they asked, come on deck and be ready

to move our vessel to a much better mooring at an unoccupied government wharf on the other side of the harbour, as soon as they had hauled her off the mud?

I thanked them but pointed out that I would never be able to find the wharf in darkness and in fog and so would prefer to moor alongside one of their draggers for the night.

They said they understood how I felt, but two of them would be delighted to pilot us across the harbour. No, they would not come aboard *Happy Adventure* in order to do this; they would pilot us from a motor boat bearing a large light and keeping well out of our way.

The kindliness of Newfoundland fishermen has to be experienced to be appreciated.

When morning dawned we found ourselves free men again. We were lying at a very long wharf built by the government in the wrong part of the harbour which is where the Newfoundland government normally builds such wharves. There was nobody else at this wharf and no houses anywhere near it. We had it all to ourselves and through the next three days kept it all to ourselves despite the arrival, because of a storm warning, of great numbers of vessels. They so crowded the fish-plant wharf that there was not room for them all and many had to anchor in the stream. Jack had the feeling we were being treated as pariahs until on the evening of the third day we were joined in exile by the *Jeannie Barnes*.

She was a slab-sided steel monstrosity, fifty or sixty feet long. She had something of the look of a seagoing power yacht but this was negated by her incredible state of dishabille. She seemed to have just escaped from the Sargasso Sea after having rusted there for many decades. Nevertheless we were delighted to have company and we hurried to take her lines. Her skipper and owner, a raffish, bearded, and slouching chap with very few teeth left in his head, but with an ingratiating smile, thanked us kindly and invited us aboard to meet the rest of the crew: his twelve-year-old, red-headed son and a nondescript, mumbling fellow who was cook, deckhand, and engineer.

The *Barnes* was not a member of the fishing fraternity. Her skipper-owner eked out a living carrying small freight consignments here and there about the coast, showing movies to outport villagers, selling patent medicines, and in general picking up a dollar anywhere and anyhow he could. Over a cup of dreadful coffee he asked us what we were doing on the wrong side of the harbour.

"How come they kicked *you* off the plant wharf, eh? Well you don't have to tell me unless you wants. They're a nasty bunch over there. They won't hardly part with a drop of gasoline on tick. Won't give a feller no credit at all. I told 'em last time I filled up there I'd pay 'em when I got the money, and one of these years I may."

Having indignantly denied that we had been kicked off (a denial which the skipper took with obvious scepticism), we invited him to come aboard our vessel. We had a new problem and we had hopes he might help us solve it.

As was so often the case aboard *Happy Adventure* it was an engine problem. The bullgine had learned how to heat herself up until she got so hot that when we tried to stop her we could not do it. Disconnecting the battery did no good because the igniter, having become incandescent, would continue to fire the gasoline charges anyway. The only way we could stop her was to turn off the gasoline tap at the main tank, and it then took up to five minutes for her to consume the gasoline remaining in her huge carburetor before she would finally give up the ghost.

She revealed this distressing new trait the day before the *Jeannie Barnes* arrived, when we made a voyage across the harbour to the wharf of a small merchant who sold fuel, food, and sundries to fishermen. His dock was crowded with small boats and so, for safety's sake, I ordered Jack to stop the engine while we were still some distance off. The engine refused to stop and we ploughed ahead at full speed. I managed to heel her over in a sharp turn, doing no more damage to the moored boats than to skin the paint off a trap skiff. Shaken to the quick, I headed the vessel back toward the centre of the harbour – whereupon the engine stopped. Naturally it would not start again.

We dropped anchor and there we lay for three hours, the cynosure of all eyes, while we waited for the engine to cool. When we eventually got it going again we crawled fearfully back to our isolation berth, not having enough courage to make another pass at the merchant's wharf.

In order to regain our mooring at the government wharf we cut off the gas while well off shore, let the engine die, and then used our little dory to tow the schooner ignominiously to her berth.

The skipper of the *Jeannie Barnes* diagnosed our trouble in a wink. "Your checks is wore out," he told us.

We politely asked what checks were and he explained tolerantly that they were small brass valves which controlled the water circulation through the cooling system.

"Where," I asked, "can we get new ones?"

"Well, I suppose you got to go to St. John's, me son. Only place you're likely to find 'em."

There seemed to be a conspiracy on foot to send us back to the grey capital of Newfoundland.

Fortunately Trepassey possessed a telegraph station from

which I dispatched a long, somewhat garbled but urgent s.o.s. to the one man in St. John's upon whom I knew I could depend. His name was Mike Donovan and he was then the Director of Provincial Library Services. While stationed in Holland after the end of the Second World War Mike Donovan stole a German v-2 rocket. After painting it blue, building a wooden conning tower on it, and brazenly calling it a one-man submarine, he shipped it back to Canada as a glorious souvenir. I felt that a man of Donovan's talents could surely help us out of our dilemma.

Mike delivered true to form. The following day, the inhabitants of Trepassey were electrified to see a small pickup truck come bucking across the caribou barrens behind the village. It made its way erratically in leaps and bounds to the government wharf. A very drunken, very Irish, very voluble little man tumbled out of it and identified himself as "a friend to old Mike, ye know."

He was also a friend to us. At considerable risk to life, limb, and his precious little truck, he delivered to us two sets of checks and the nine bottles remaining out of the case of rum Mike had entrusted to him.

We did not grudge the little man his cut. He had earned it fair and square.

The skipper of the *Jeannie Barnes* shared some of the rum with us and in turn repaired our engine and presented us with several very old and incredibly dirty charts. He also gave us compass courses designed to keep us clear of Cape St. Mary's and to assist us in crossing the wide mouth of mighty Placentia Bay although, as he unnecessarily pointed out:

"They won't be all that much good to you without you find a compass better'n that bate-up old piece of junk *you* got."

Despite his pessimism about our chances, we were grateful to him and we were sorry to see him go when, late one afternoon, he cast off his lines and his boat went grumbling off into the fog, trusting to her battered radar set to show her the way to her next port-of-call.

We never saw her or her crew again. Three weeks later the *Jeannie Barnes* was missing. The body of the red-headed little boy was picked up in a cod net a few miles off the Southern Shore. The bodies of the skipper and the mate were never found. The *Barnes* had been returning to St. John's in heavy fog, with her old radar out of order, when she disappeared.

Probably she was cut down by a foreign dragger which had been taking advantage of the fog to fish inside the three-mile limit – but only the unanswering sea will ever know what really happened.

10 · *The foggy, foggy dew*

WE SPENT five days waiting for good weather before reaching the conclusion that to wait was vain. Good weather and Trepassey did not go together.

So early on the sixth day we cast off our lines, started the bullgine, and steamed off into the fog. We now had a definite destination in mind, if not in view. We had given up our original intention of sailing to the tropics because it was clear from a scrutiny of our log that, even if we maintained our current rate of progress, it would take us sixteen months to reach the Caribbean; twenty-nine months to reach the Azores; and seven and a half years to reach the South Pacific. We did not have that much time. Consequently we chose as our alternative the island of St. Pierre.

While hardly tropical in character, and able to boast of no brown-skinned *wahines*, this little island did offer certain compensations. It was a foreign land, flying the French flag. It was, and remains, famous for having the cheapest and most abundant supply of alcohol to be found anywhere on or near the North American continent. But perhaps St. Pierre's greatest attraction for us was that it lay no more than one hundred and twenty miles to the westward of Trepassey and only a few miles off the south coast of Newfoundland. We felt we had at least a chance of reaching St. Pierre before winter closed in upon us.

Visibility in Trepassey harbour itself was surprisingly good as we set out. We *almost* saw the fish plant, and we certainly knew where it was because the wind was blowing from it to us. Once, as we thundered through the harbour channel, we caught an indistinct glimpse of land off the port bow. It may have been Powles Head, the entry landmark. If so, it was the last landmark we were to see for a long time to come.

Trepassey Bay was black with fog. We had gone no more than a mile when, faint-heart that I am, I decided it would be hopeless to proceed.

"Jack," I said as firmly as I could, "we'll have to put back to harbour. There isn't a chance we're going to find St. Pierre in fog like this. Considering the state of that bleeding compass, we're more likely to end up in Ireland instead."

Jack fixed me with a cold stare and there was no mistaking the threat of mutiny in his voice:

"The hell you say! Mowat, if you turn back now I swear I'll do an Enos. I'll leave you to rot in Trepassey harbour to the end of your born days! Besides, you silly bastard, how do you think you're going to *find* Trepassey again? I'm going below to work out a course to clear Cape Pine. You keep this boat heading as she is or else . . . !"

He vanished and I was alone with my thoughts. I had to admit he had a point. Although we had found Trepassey harbour once in heavy fog we weren't likely to be as lucky a second time, and the rocks and reefs on both sides of the entrance were particularly fearsome and unforgiving. Also I was pretty sure Jack would make good his threat, supposing we did regain the harbour, and the prospect of being marooned alone with *Happy Adventure* in Trepassey was too horrible to contemplate. The lesser of two evils would be to continue out to sea. I held the little vessel "steady as she goes," but with my free hand I pulled out my own personal bottle of rum from its hiding place in the lazaret, and poured a good dollop overboard for the Old Man. *Happy Adventure* puttered blindly on into the dark and brooding murk and I was soon fog-chilled, unutterably lonely, and scared to death. Since rum is a known and accepted antidote for all three conditions I took a long, curative drink for each separate ailment. By the time Jack reappeared on deck I was much easier in my mind.

By 1000 hours we had run the required distance to clear Cape Pine (distance run was measured on an ancient brass patent log towed astern of the vessel), and were ready to alter course to the northwest, to begin the twenty-mile crossing of the mouth of St. Mary's Bay. But now a problem arose – we did not have the faintest idea what our compass error was on such a course. All we could do was alter ninety degrees to the north and hope we were actually sailing northwest despite what the compass had to say about it.

The knowledge that we were by then in close proximity to St. Shotts did nothing to bring me peace of mind. Having once been to St. Shotts by land, as a visitor, I had no desire to return to it unexpectedly by sea, as a piece of business. The bare possibility gave me such a bad attack of shivering that I had to send Jack down below to check the pumps while I took another cure.

It was a curious thing, but whenever I felt a pressing need to reach for the bottle Jack seemed perfectly willing, and even anxious, to nip below and give me privacy. Sometimes he even anticipated my need. At the time I thought this was only happy coincidence. But at the conclusion of the passage when I was cleaning up in the engine room, I found, under a pile of rags, a bottle that was the twin of the one I kept hidden in the lazaret. Like mine, it was completely empty.

The crossing of St. Mary's Bay began uneventfully. There was not a breath of wind. There was very little sensation of movement because there were no reference points for the eye to find. We seemed poised and immobile in the centre of a bowl of calm and leaden water a hundred feet or so in circumference.

This was a region where we knew we could expect to encounter other vessels, particularly draggers and fishing schooners, with the consequent danger of collisions. Being without radar we had to rely on other boats to spot us and keep out of our way. Nor could we have heard their fog-horns above the roar of the bullgine. We ourselves did not need a fog-horn – the engine made more noise than any horn could have done.

Just after noon the fog to starboard suddenly grew black as the shadowy shape of a vessel came into view about fifty yards away. She was a big power schooner on a converging course with us and her rail was lined with gesticulating figures.

We were so glad to see other human beings in this void that we ran close alongside and stopped our engine. The big schooner did likewise and the two vessels drifted side by side.

"Where you bound, Skipper?" someone called across to us.

"St. Pierre," I cried back. "Heading to clear Cape St. Mary's with a five-mile offing."

There was a long thoughtful silence from our neighbour. And then:

"Well, byes, I don't see how you're going to do it steering the course you is. Unless, that is, you plans to take her up the Branch River, carry her over the Platform Hills, and put her on a railroad train. If I was you, I'd haul off to port about nine points. Good luck to ye!"

The diesels of the big vessel started with a roar and she pulled clear of us and disappeared.

We altered *ten* points to the southward just to be sure. The lubber line on the compass now indicated we were steaming south into the open ocean on a course for Bermuda. As the hours went by we found this increasingly unsettling to the mind. Was the schooner skipper correct, or was he wrong? The compass insisted he was very wrong indeed. We stewed over the matter until mid-afternoon, by which time we had lost all confidence in compass, schooner skipper, and ourselves.

At this juncture the bullgine took our minds off our navigational problems. It gave a tremendous belch. A huge cloud of blue smoke burst out of the companionway. I plunged below and grabbed for the fire extinguisher, expecting to find the entire engine room aflame. However all that had happened was that the exhaust stack had blown off at its junction with the engine, allowing exhaust gases and bits of white-hot carbon to fill the little cabin. The engine continued to run, if anything, a little better, since there was no back pressure from the stack.

There was also no longer anything between the hot exhaust and the bilges of the boat in which floated a thin but ever present scum of gasoline.

I held my breath, screwed my eyes tight shut, groped for the ignition wire, and pulled it off. Then I fled back on deck.

The bullgine wheezed to a stop and Jack and I sat in the

ensuing, overwhelming silence and discussed our situation. It was not a cheerful prospect that we faced.

There was no way we could repair the exhaust stack without access to a welding torch. There was no wind and we could not sail, and so without the engine we would be doomed to sit where we were until something happened. That might be a long time but when something *did* happen we could be pretty sure it would be the wrong thing. There was apparently nothing for it but to restart the engine and hope she would not backfire and blow us all to Kingdom Come.

Leaving me to cogitate upon the problem Jack took advantage of the silence to slip below and turn on our small battery radio in an attempt to get a weather forecast. We could not use this radio while the engine was running because it was impossible to hear the tinny, indistinct sound that came out of it. Now, by pressing his ear against the speaker, Jack could hear the strains of cowboy music from Marystown Radio across Placentia Bay. Because it served a fishing community Marystown Radio gave the weather at frequent intervals.

Happy Adventure lay as silent as a painted ship upon a painted ocean – one painted in unrelieved tones of grey. After five or ten minutes Jack reappeared on deck.

"Farley," he said quietly, too quietly, "you aren't going to want to believe this, but they're putting out a general storm warning. There's a tropical storm coming in from the south-west and it's due here in ten hours, more or less. They're predicting winds of sixty knots!"

We got out the charts, spread them on the deck, and pored over them. First Jack would pour, then I would pour. This made us feel better, but it did not do us a great deal of practical good because we did not know exactly where we were. In truth, we didn't have a clue as to where we were. However assuming we had cleared Cape St. Mary's and were crossing the mouth of Placentia Bay – a fifty-mile-wide traverse – we found by the chart that we could not be less than

eighty miles from St. Pierre. Under full engine power *Happy Adventure* could manage five knots. In ten hours' time this would have put us thirty miles short of the haven of St. Pierre and we knew that if the tropical storm arrived on schedule, thirty miles might just as well be three hundred.

The nearest port in which we could hope to find shelter appeared to be Placentia Harbour, twenty-five or thirty miles to the northward of Cape St. Mary's, on the east coast of the great bay.

I was rather afraid to suggest we try for Placentia Harbour, expecting another mutinous response from Jack. But he appeared to have had his fill of excitement, and he agreed that, yes, perhaps we should put in there for the night.

He went below and cautiously started the bullgine. We reset the patent log to zero and put the vessel on what we trusted (trust was all we had) was the correct course for Placentia Harbour.

It grew bitter cold and the fog began to close in tighter and tighter until it was so black that, had my watch not denied it, we could have believed night had fallen. Jack and I huddled together in the steering well, as far away from the engine room as we could get. We had also taken the precaution of hauling the dory up close under the stern so we could leap directly aboard it in an emergency; and we had stowed the dory with our last communal bottle of rum and a bag of sea biscuits. There was no room for anything else and, indeed, there was no room for us if it should come to that. We hoped it wouldn't come to that.

Five hours later the patent log showed we had run the proper distance to Placentia. I sent Jack to stop the bullgine so we could listen for the fog-horn at the harbour mouth.

Then a strange thing happened. The engine stopped but the roar continued. At first I thought this must be a physiological reaction of my ears and mind to the endless thunder of the bullgine which we had endured for so many hours, but suddenly the truth came clear to me.

"Start her, Jack! Start her! Oh start her, Jack!" I howled.

Startled, Jack did as he was told and the bullgine caught on the first spin of the flywheel. I shoved the tiller over, hard. *Happy Adventure* picked up way and turned westward, away from the roaring surf that lay unseen but not unheard a few yards off her starboard bow.

We ran for half an hour before I could relax my grip on the tiller, unclamp my jaws, swallow once or twice, and find my voice again.

We had no way of knowing how close we had come to Placentia Harbour itself, but we did know we had come much too close to the east coast of the great bay. We knew we did not want to encounter it again under any conceivable circumstances. So we held on to the westward, knowing we had at least forty or fifty miles of open water ahead of us in that direction. We did not allow ourselves to think beyond those forty or fifty miles.

As we drove away from the land a kind of peace came over us. The bullgine rumbled and the exhaust smoke rolled out of the cabin into our faces. The fog grew thicker and somewhere the sun sank below the horizon, and it was night. We did not bother lighting our oil-burning navigation lights, because they could not have been seen from more than four or five feet away. We sat in our oilskins and blundered on into an infinity of blackness; into a void that had no end. We told each other that this was how the mariners of ancient times, the Norse in their longships, the Basques in their cranky vessels, Columbus in his caravel, must have felt as they ran their westing down toward a dark unknown. Day after day, night after night, they must have learned how to live with the terrors of a long uncertainty. On that black night perhaps we shared a little of what they must have felt.

At midnight Jack got another forecast. The spiralling storm centre had slowed down and was not expected to reach our area until just before dawn. In preparation for its arrival we double-reefed the main and foresail and felt our way over every inch of the fog-shrouded vessel putting all things in order for a blow.

A light breeze had risen from southerly, so we hoisted sail and shut down the bullgine, which had again begun to misbehave. The new checks had not bedded properly in their seats and she had started to overheat again; thus increasing the likelihood of backfires and of even more spectacular pyrotechnics.

We slipped along under sail in almost perfect silence in a world reduced to a diameter of not more than fifteen feet. I worked at the pump and Jack, at the helm, leaned over the compass whose card was lit by the dim glow of an expiring flashlight which we had taped to the binnacle, in lieu of a proper lamp.

The thought occurred to me that if we *had* to find ourselves in a situation of some jeopardy, we were better off aboard *Happy Adventure* than aboard a well-found, comfortable, and properly equipped yacht.

"You have to be kidding!" Jack said when I propounded this idea.

"Not at all. Look at it this way. If we were in a hundred-thousand-dollar yacht we'd have to worry like hell about the prospect of losing her. We don't have that worry aboard *Happy Adventure*. We only have to worry about losing ourselves and she doesn't give us any *time* to worry about that." I paused to let this sink in. Then: "Would you mind unstrapping that flashlight from the binnacle and bringing it below? The main pump has jammed again."

By the time we had repaired the pump and regained control over the leaks the little vessel had developed a new motion. She was beginning to roll. A heavy swell was heaving in from seaward. It gradually built up until we were rolling and pitching hard enough to spill the small wind out of our sails. Booms, gaffs, and blocks charged about, banging and thumping unseen above our heads.

The wind now failed and we lay becalmed on the black, heaving sea in an ominous silence broken only by the complaining noises of our running gear. There was nothing for it but to lower away and risk starting the bullgine once more.

She started with extreme reluctance, but she started, and for once her horrible outcry was welcome music in our ears. We drove on into the hours of the graveyard watch, hauling the patent log every now and again, to make sure we were not closing too fast with the alien coast which lay somewhere

off our bows. At 0300 hours the log showed thirty-five miles and, very mindful of our recent experience off Placentia, we decided to stop the bullgine and listen.

At first we heard nothing – then very distant and indistinct we caught the faint moan of a diaphone. We were no longer alone in an empty world.

Each diaphone (fog-horn) has its own signature or code by which it can be identified. One may be timed to blow three five-second blasts at three-second intervals at the beginning of every minute; its nearest neighbour may be timed to blow for ten seconds, every thirty seconds. Jack slipped below to get the official Light and Fog-horn List while I began timing the distant moans. This was difficult because fog has the ability to muffle, distort, and freakishly obliterate sounds. Furthermore the second hand on my watch had a disconcerting way of moving in swift rushes followed by intervals of extreme sluggishness. Jack's watch was not available because some hours earlier the bullgine had struck it a smart blow with the starting handle.

Our first identification of the horn suggested it was on Cape Ann at the entrance to Gloucester, Massachusetts. We did not believe this, so we tried again. The next identification was of Red Rock at the mouth of the Saguenay in the St. Lawrence River; we did not believe that one either. Finally by the slow process of elimination we concluded that the horn *might* be on Little Burin Island on the west side of Placentia Bay.

Having perhaps located Little Burin Island, our next problem was to get into Burin harbour. The Newfoundland Pilot Book informed us that the harbour was complicated, with off-lying dangers, and that it should *not* be entered unless one took aboard a pilot. Furthermore it should *not* be entered, even in daylight, unless one possessed local knowledge. The book said nothing about what should *not* be done at night, in a black fog, by perfect strangers. We drew our own conclusions.

We decided we had better stay where we were until

dawn. If the storm struck before then we would have no alternative but to head out to sea and try to ride it out. If the storm held off until dawn, and if the fog lightened, there would be a chance of closing with the shore without inviting certain disaster. There was the further possibility that we might encounter a shore-based fishing boat from which we could get a little "local knowledge."

According to my watch dawn arrived at 0600 hours, but there was little visual evidence of its coming. True, the fog lightened enough so that we could actually see each other if we stood no farther than six feet apart. A kind of sepulchral semi-luminosity made it possible to read the compass card without the flashlight, which was just as well because the flashlight batteries had burned out and we had no replace- ments. At first we suspected that my watch was wrong (and we hoped it was), but when an early rising puffin suddenly whirred through the murk and just managed to avoid collid- ing with our mainmast, we knew that dawn had really come.

For half an hour more we waited, hoping to hear the slow, measured throb of fishing-boat engines. During the hours of drifting the current had carried us closer to shore and the horn was now quite distinct, and it was unmistakably Little Burin. Yet the fishermen of Burin did not seem to be abroad and at their work. We cursed them for being sluggards until Jack remembered that – storm warnings aside – this was Sun- day morning. We thereupon gave up hoping for salvation from the fishermen. Being good Christian men they were all ashore seeing to their own salvation.

At seven o'clock we did hear a new noise. It was the first keening note of wind in our rigging. It was the first breath of the oncoming storm.

The skipper of the *Jeannie Barnes* had given us a small-scale and much-worn chart of Placentia Bay. Although it was almost indecipherable at least it told us there were no reefs or rocks off shore from Little Burin Island itself. In our dilemma we now decided to run straight toward the horn and, when we had it close aboard, swing north and try to feel our way behind the island. We would anchor there in whatever shelter we could find until the gale was over or until the fog blew away allowing us to seek a better haven.

The approach run was a ghastly ordeal. In order to keep track of the horn we had to stop the engine every five or ten minutes so that we could take a bearing; each time we stopped her she became more difficult to start. At eight-thirty, when we had worked our way within a quarter of a mile of the horn, the engine absolutely refused to start again. I sweated over it, exchanging igniters and frigging with wires, while the sound of the surf breaking on the two-hundred-foot-high seaward cliffs of Little Burin Island grew steadily louder as the tide carried us toward shore.

It took almost an hour to revive the bullgine and we knew we would not be able to risk stopping her again until we had reached an anchorage. Jack went forward to the bowsprit while I steered. I could only just see him as he waved his arm to signal the direction of the horn, which he could hear even above the thunder of the engine. Suddenly he flung up both arms at once. Confused, I put the helm hard over. *Happy Adventure* spun on her heel and we headed back out to sea.

Jack stumbled aft, a shaken man. He told me that as he stared into the murk the grey wall had suddenly turned pitch black, not only dead ahead, but off to port and starboard too. It took him only a fraction of an instant to realize that he was staring at the shrouded face of cliffs which loomed no more than a few yards from him. Since destruction seemed certain no matter which way we turned he tried to signal to me to stop the engine and so at least ease the final blow when *Happy Adventure* struck. Luck was with us. We had entered a shallow bay to the south of the fog-horn and it was just wide enough to let us turn about and make our escape.

Our immediate reaction was to give up any further attempts to reach shelter and to decide to take our chances with the storm at sea. However a little reflection changed our minds. *Happy Adventure* was leaking so badly that the unreliable pump was barely able to hold its own. The engine was clearly on its last legs. The wind was rising out of the sou'east. We knew we would stand no chance of beating off shore into the teeth of mounting wind and seas. One way or another we seemed destined to go ashore; only the choice of how we did it still remained to us.

We chose to make another pass at Little Burin Island.

Jack went forward again. He told me afterwards that he had an almost irresistible impulse to pick up our boat-hook and to stand poised on the bow with the pole thrust out ahead of him to fend us off the cliffs. It was not such a crazy idea as it sounds. A few days later the light-keeper told me *his* impressions of our tilt with Little Burin Island.

"I heard you fellas out there fer hours and hours. Couldn't make out what you was about. Heard your engine fer a time, then she'd shut off and I'd think you was gone away or gone ashore. Then, bang, you'd be coming at me again. Well, Sir, the last time you come in I thought you'd come right up the cliffs, gone by my door, and fair into my back yard."

On our final approach our course was indeed dead at the horn. I could even hear it from where I sat at the helm; a bull's bellow above the blatting of the engine. Jack's right arm shot out and I hauled the tiller hard to port. This time I too saw the black loom as we ran parallel to the cliff and not more than a ship's length from it. The horn suddenly boomed, and it was straight overhead. I hauled harder on the stick and the black loom vanished and we were again lost in the world of fog.

That was the way we navigated. I eased the stick over very slowly. As soon as the fog began to darken Jack would wave me off. As the fog lightened and we lost touch with the island, we would turn cautiously inward again until we raised its loom before hauling off once more. Despite the chill of the morning I was sweating like a pig. I was so engrossed that it was some time before I realized that the boom of the horn was now behind me. We had rounded the corner of the island and were running down its northern shore.

I had the chart spread out on my knee and I peered at it

trying to make out the water depths behind the island. Eventually I read part of a line of soundings. They showed twelve fathoms right to the foot of the cliffs – and we had just fifteen fathoms of anchor chain.

Up forward Jack was already flaking the chain on deck, ready for my order to let go the hook. I yelled to him and he came aft. I showed him the soundings. We both knew there was no way we were going to ride out a storm with only three fathoms of scope on our chain. Then Jack grinned. A terrible grin.

"The hell!" he said. "Head her north. We'll run right up Burin Inlet. We'll hold tight up against the western shore and steer by the loom of the land."

And that is what we did. Fired with an exhilaration that might have been recklessness, or may have just been the fine feeling of already having done the impossible, we ran up Burin Inlet for almost two miles. We never saw a thing. We ran solely by the loom of the black fog on our port bow. When we had run far enough to feel we were as safe as we could ever hope to be we stopped the engine.

Happy Adventure drifted through the grey soup on calm, still waters. Somewhere a dog barked. Somewhere a church bell was ringing. Jack swung the lead over the bows and got four fathoms with a mud bottom. The anchor went over and the chain ran out with a clear, strong song.

After a while we descended into our little cabin and went to sleep.

11 · *The boys of Burin*

I WOKE about noon; woke suddenly and filled with unease. I had been dreaming I was in command of the *Queen Mary* trying to make Burin harbour. All the windows on her bridge were painted black, I was wearing dark glasses, and it was a pitch black, foggy night, and . . . .

I woke, and the cabin was streaming with sunlight. *Happy Adventure* was tugging at her anchor, and a slop was banging against her bows, giving her life and motion. The wind was wheening through her rigging and a halyard was snapping sharply against the mast.

I got sleepily out of my bunk, went aft and pumped for an hour then, duty done, crawled up on deck.

It was a stupendous day, brilliant and vibrant. The gale was snorting high around the surrounding hills, whipping torn clouds across an azure sky, but down in the long gleaming arm of the inlet there was no more than a fresh breeze. Of fog there was never a trace. Of life and people, there was evidence in plenty.

We were anchored on the edge of a fleet of trap skiffs, swamps (small rowboats), seagoing dories, and two small coastal schooners. One big skiff was swinging at her moorings only twenty yards astern of us. A quarter of a mile to the eastward lay a little village of brightly painted houses, neat flakes and stages, and a tidy wooden church. Sitting in the white sunlight on the end of a small dock were five or six children patiently fishing for sculpins. A frieze of gaily dressed men and women moved along the shore road between their houses and the church. *And there was no fish plant anywhere in sight.*

Jack joined me, red-eyed, dirty-faced, and tousle-headed (I do not know how *I* looked since we had no mirror on board), and together we welcomed our first visitor. He was an elderly man wearing his Sunday best and slowly rowing a dory toward us. When he came alongside he turned his head to take in the whole of our little vessel.

"Marnin', Skipper," he said finally. "Come in through the fog?"

I admitted that we had.

"Well now," he said and spat neatly into the water. "Come in through the fog, eh? Been up the inlet many times afore?"

I said we had never been in Burin Inlet before. And then he gave us our accolade.

"Don't know as I ever seed a thicker nor a blacker fog. Don't know as I'd a cared to bring a vessel in through it meself."

We acknowledged this high compliment by inviting him to come aboard but he refused. Instead he invited us to come ashore, assuring us that his Woman would be proud to give us Sunday dinner. When we tried to decline on the grounds that we were filthy dirty and had no clean clothing he would have none of it. Telling us he would be back in an hour's time he rowed away without a backward glance.

Such was our welcome to Burin Inlet and it was the beginning of one of the warmest and most enjoyable human associations I can recall. The people of Burin Inlet do not have many peers in this cold world of ours.

Unhappily, Jack could not remain to enjoy their hospitality. There was a telephone at Burin Cove and, foolishly, he used it to call Toronto. Instantly a flood of pressing business problems was unleashed through the slender wire and Jack, indomitable in the face of natural challenge, wilted under it. For him the voyage was over, temporarily, at least. The following morning he climbed aboard an ancient car for the long run back to St. John's over the almost non-existent Burin Peninsula Highway. Much depressed and considerably unmanned by thoughts of his departure, I wanted to go with him, but he would have none of that.

"You damn well stay aboard," he told me in his naval tone of voice. "I'll talk Mike Donovan into coming down to join you. Poor fellow, he won't know any better. And then the two of you take the boat to St. Pierre. You can leave her there if you want to, but she goes to St. Pierre where I can rejoin her sometime later on. You hear?"

I heard and reluctantly agreed. I felt somewhat guilty.

The voyage had hardly turned out to be the pleasure cruise Jack had anticipated. Nevertheless it had not been a total loss. When I rowed back aboard after saying goodbye I found he had left something behind. Hanging in the eyes of the ship, like a modern version of a baronial coat-of-mail, was Jack's steel and elastic corset. Whatever damage *Happy Adventure* had inflicted on his spirit, she had at least made him forget about his aching back.

The days that followed were unbelievably peaceful and pleasant. I acquired a following of boys, almost all of them with the surname Moulton, and these were, in the vernacular, "right smart lads." Whenever I undertook a task, whether it was painting decks, reaving new rigging, or repacking the shaft housing, they were on hand to help. It frequently turned out they knew more about the work than I did, and not infrequently they turned me into a loafer with nothing to do but watch while they did my work.

When I encountered problems which neither the boys nor I could handle the men of the inlet came to the rescue. One of them made a three-hour trip in his dory to find a welder and a welding outfit to repair the exhaust pipe. Another noticed I had no hawse pipe and that the anchor chain was cutting a deep groove in the rail. This man, also a Moulton, excavated a hawse pipe from someone's store, brought it to the ship, and installed it with consummate workmanship – without even being asked.

On my second day in Burin Cove the gale grew worse and swung around on shore, so that *Happy Adventure* was in some danger of dragging her anchor. Whereupon two men rowed out, came shyly aboard, and volunteered to help me take the vessel across the inlet to the better protection afforded by Spoon Cove. That evening, after we had moved her, a ten-year-old boy rowed right across the inlet through a heavy chop to bring me my laundry which his mother had, out of the kindness of her heart, done for me at Burin Cove.

When she left Muddy Hole, *Happy Adventure* was in a disgraceful state of dirt, incomplete painting, and general dishabille. Her arduous voyage had not improved her appearance, but after a few days in Spoon Cove she began to look more like a ship. She glistened with fresh paint. Her cabin, scrubbed and polished, looked clean and ceased to smell like an abandoned abattoir.

Even the bullgine was painted, after first submitting to the cunning ministrations of old Uncle John Moulton, who knew more about make-and-break engines than their designer ever did. Uncle John made her go; and he sweet-talked her so she would go for me and go when she was asked.

I grew fat in Spoon Cove. Every family there seemed anxious that I should have at least one meal with them, and when I grew bloated and invented excuses to stay aboard at mealtime, it did me little good. A timid knock on the cabin trunk would announce the arrival of a teen-age girl bearing a napkin-covered dish of hot fish-and-brewis, fresh baked cod, stewed bake-apples (the Newfoundland name for cloud-berries), or a repast equally delectable.

In the evenings the men would come aboard and yarn. Two or three of them would sit in the little cabin and talk, slowly, with long pauses, about their lives and their futures. They had lived good lives. Successful fishermen, they had built substantial houses, which their wives kept immaculate; houses fitted with running water, bathrooms, and other modern conveniences. They owned large, elaborate, fish stores with big net lofts over them; good sturdy stages, and fine seagoing boats which they built themselves from timber cut during the long winter months back "in the country."

However there was an undercurrent of bewilderment and even fear in their voices. The policies of the new (post-Confederation) Newfoundland government, directed toward an unsuccessful attempt to convert the sea-girt island to a mainland-type industrial economy, were spelling the death of the fisheries which had sustained the Islanders through five centuries. It was becoming increasingly difficult to make a living from the sea. Grown men still stuck to it, but for the youngsters, including the lads who had adopted me, there was now no future except emigration to the mainland of Canada.

One of the men remembered how, shortly after the then-and-forever Premier, Joseph Smallwood, came to power, he told the people of the Island to burn their stages, haul out their boats, and throw away their gear because, "you will never have to go fishing again. There will be jobs ashore for every one of you!"

"Ten year gone by since then," the fisherman mused, his face dark and intent in the dim light of my oil lamp. "Ten year, and the jobs he promised was all made of air and foam. 'Twas a good thing for we, we never heeded what he said, else we'd have been in the same boat with t'ousands of out-port fellers that has to live upon the dole.

"We'uns in Burin Inlet, we kept our boats and our gear and we still catches fish as good as ever we did. But we gets no price for fish these days."

"Aye," added one of his companions. "The fish is still there in plenty, byes. If Joey had spent all the millions he wasted on rubber plants and candy factories helpin' we fellers build deepsea vessels like the Norwegians has, we'd be well found today."

"Jobs!" said a third man bitterly. "The only jobs he's found for we, is diggin' our own graves!"

It was disturbing to listen to these men and to see them being brought to defeat and to despair. Nevertheless the out-port life was not yet dead in Spoon Cove. During my days there I tasted what, to me, seemed an almost idyllic existence and I savoured every moment of it.

There was the day we barked *Happy Adventure*'s canvas.

Barking is an ancient process whereby nets are soaked in a boiling-hot mixture of sea water, cod-liver oil, tar, and a natural resin. Barking stops the nets from rotting when under water and prevents mildew when they are stored ashore; it was often used in the past on schooner sails as well as on the nets. When properly done, barking dyes the canvas a rich red-brown, and a man can leave his sails untended through weeks of rain and fog and never have them harmed.

A few days before I arrived at Spoon Cove the fishermen had gathered together for a communal barking of their nets and the barking kettle, an immense iron cauldron holding well over a hundred gallons, was still full of the malodorous barking mixture called "cutch." I was invited to make use of it, and two fourteen-year-olds, Alan and Gerald Moulton, volunteered to organize the job for me.

The next dawn I was awakened by a peculiarly pungent smell wafting into the cabin. When I came on deck the land-wash was obscured under a pall of black smoke. The boys were busy on shore. They had lit a great fire under the barking pot and were feeding it with masses of "condemned" tarred netting. A few hundred feet above them on the slope two red-faced and indignant ladies were screeching at the boys. This was laundry day and their lines of clothing were rapidly turning a sooty grey. The boys paid not the slightest heed, and the ladies (Newfoundland ladies always know when they are beaten) took in their laundry and vanished indoors to await a more propitious hour.

While the cutch heated up, a platoon of boys scrambled over the vessel unbending her sails. These were then carried to a vast flake, used in other times for drying fish, where they were spread out under the hot summer sun.

Then the fun began. Six boys armed with buckets commuted back and forth between the great pot and the flake. Pails of scalding cutch were poured on the canvas and the liquid was vigorously scrubbed in with birch brooms. Within an hour everything in sight had turned dark red. The boys looked like the reincarnation of a tribe of Beothuk Indians — the aboriginal inhabitants of Newfoundland. The very sea itself along the land-wash turned a rusty brown. I sat apart in idleness and watched with awe as the boys scampered about in clouds of steam, yelling like banshees and working like red devils.

It was a very hot day and by the time they had emptied the pot the boys were ready for a break. One of them rather

shyly asked if I would like to join them for a swim. I liked
–so they led me off up the slope behind the harbour to
their favourite pond. It was a long hike through stunted
spruce groves, over bare rock outcrops, and up stony draws
to the very crest of the highest hill. The pond was shallow
and warmed by the sun to a comfortable temperature. We all
stripped off and splashed about for a while until Alan and
one of the other lads produced willow rods from a hiding
place in the grass and started fishing. I thought this must be
wishful thinking on their part for a less fishy place I have
seldom seen. However they immediately began hauling in
good sized speckled trout. "Mud trout" *they* called them. By
whatever name, they tasted sweet enough when I sat down
to a mess of them for my supper late that night.

I had almost decided I would be content to spend the rest
of the summer, if not the rest of my life, in Spoon Cove when
Mike Donovan arrived, brimming with energy and with
enthusiasm. The idyll was at an end. Once more I had to face
the prospect of continuing my voyage upon the grey, im-
placable seas.

I faced it with some reservations. Chief amongst these
was Mike. He was hardly what one would call a seasoned
mariner. To the best of his own recollection he had only been
upon the waters three times in his life. The later voyages
consisted of ocean crossings in troopships during the war.
The first took place when, at the age of six, he ventured out
on a pond in a Toronto park on a makeshift raft. He fell off,
but was rescued by a mounted policeman who rode his horse
full gallop into the pond to snatch Mike from an early grave.
Apart from these occasions his experience with the sea and
with boats was nil. This did not bother Mike, who was the
world's greatest optimist, but it tended to disturb me a trifle.

Mike had driven down to Spoon Cove from St. John's in
a Volkswagen. He now proceeded to remove from it two of
the largest suitcases I have ever seen. How he had crammed
them into his little car I cannot guess. One of them would
have filled *Happy Adventure*'s cabin to the exclusion of any

human beings. Gaily he flung these on the deck and flung
himself after them. Mike was a natural born flinger; long,
lean, lanky, and exuberant.

"What in hell are you doing with those suitcases? What's
in them?" I asked, appalled.

"Library supplies. You think I'm Director of Libraries for
nothing? I swung this trip by telling the Minister of Education I was going to establish a branch library system on the
sou'west coast of Newfoundland. You wouldn't want to
make a liar out of me, would you now?"

"No," I said, "I wouldn't want to do that, Mike. So just

consider you've established your first branch library right here, in Tom Moulton's fish store. Now get those goddamn trunks off my deck before you sink the boat!"

Amiability was one of Mike's strong points. Whistling cheerfully, he carted the suitcases into the fish store and stowed them behind a pile of salt cod. He returned aboard and folded himself into the cabin but not before he had produced four bottles of Big Dipper rum. Library supplies in Newfoundland obviously run to better things than paste and date-due slips.

I considered it would be wise to give Mike a crash course in seamanship before departing from Burin. And this turned out to be one of the best entertainments ever staged in Spoon Cove.

Before the course was well advanced it had drawn an audience of many small boys and girls, a dozen elderly gentlemen, and a motley crowd of fishermen. They lined the stages on both sides of us, and watched in silence as I took Mike all around the vessel, pointing out and naming everything of importance. He followed alertly, nodding his head and repeating the names after me. Since he had studied several languages and could speak at least three of them fluently he had no trouble memorizing names. I then ran him through such standard procedures as making sail, lowering sail, handling the sheets, letting go the anchor, putting the fenders overside. He was very good at it.

The audience, which had not previously suspected there was a man alive who knew as little about a boat as did Mike, began to take to him. Finally I ordered him to go aft, unship the dory from its cradle and launch it overboard.

He performed this task almost flawlessly. Almost. He erred only in looping the dory painter around his wrist before shoving the little boat over the schooner's side.

The dory's momentum shot her away from the vessel—and Mike went too, on the end of the painter. He came to the surface somewhat wild-eyed, for the water was bitter cold, and staring about as if in search of a policeman riding a horse. Alas, there was not one such in all of Burin. So he paddled to the dory, caught it, threw an arm and a leg over its side – and turned the little boat completely upside down on top of himself.

We could hear him underneath it, where he was clinging to a thwart. He was bellowing what I am afraid may have been Irish oaths but they were so muffled we could not really make them out. He was also kicking energetically with his feet and this had the effect of slowly propelling the upturned boat out into the harbour. It looked like some huge sea-tortoise, shorn of its head, although it did not sound like one.

One of the boys had by this time recovered sufficient control of himself to climb into a swamp and go in pursuit. He was unable to get Mike out from under so he towed the dory back to shore. In due time Mike's feet encountered the bottom. He ducked down and at last emerged shivering and blue into the light of day.

It would not have been surprising if he had given up the voyage there and then, climbed into his little car, and scuttled off for home. Not Mike. As he waded up on the shore he put on his broadest smile and his broadest Irish accent:

"Faith and begorra! And wouldn't that be a fine rig for swimmin' in the rain?"

The people of Spoon Cove took him to their hearts, and so did I.

There was one distinct advantage to Mike's ignorance of the sea and vessels. He did not know enough about them to be nervous. In his eyes *Happy Adventure* was the staunchest little vessel that had ever lived. He trusted her absolutely. He kept on trusting her, too, even when she did her best to disillusion him. Not, mind you, that he failed to take precautions. As he climbed into his bunk that first night he delayed a moment – to hammer a huge St. Christopher medal to the plank above his head.

Although I am not a member of Mike's faith that medal

is still where he placed it. *Somebody* must have had an eye on us in the days that followed. Whether it was St. Christopher or the Old Man of the Sea remains a mystery. I suspect it took both of them, working as a team, to do the job.

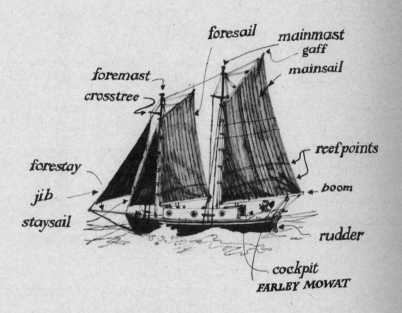

12 · *A basking shark and*
a Basque proposal

Two days after Mike's arrival we set sail for St. Pierre, which lay fifty miles to the westward around the tip of the projecting boot of the Burin Peninsula. I hopefully looked forward to an easy passage. Since it was to be a coastwise voyage within sight of land, I did not expect the eccentricities of the compass would be a problem. The engine was working better than it had ever worked before. The leaks seemed to have settled down or, at any rate, they were not beyond control of Mike's muscular abilities. We were well stored with food and rum. Even the weather forecast was good.

The forecast called for "southerly winds, light at dawn, increasing to southeast twenty; visibility four miles, except in fog." The phrase, "except in fog," occurred in every weather forecast during every voyage I ever made in six years' residence on the south coast of Newfoundland. The fog itself also occurred on every voyage except one. Sometimes the fog was in patches only a few miles wide. Usually it was rather more impressive, extending over several hundred thousand square miles of ocean. Although the weather forecasts were quite often wrong about other things they were seldom wrong about the fog.

In honour of this, his first sail, I served Mike a special breakfast. It began with oatmeal porridge and condensed milk in which several rashers of fat-back bacon bobbed. This was followed by boiled rounders. Rounders are another Newfoundland delicacy. They are very small cod that have been sun-dried "in the round," rather than split, as are the larger fish. They have a flavour and aroma rather like old cheddar cheese. Mike, who was not a born Newfoundlander, had never tasted them before, but he was game and he ate two. He agreed about the aroma and the taste, only *he* said it was more like *Gorgonzola*.

We got away from Spoon Cove at seven o'clock with just enough breeze to fill our sails and make for a brave departure. An hour later we rounded Little Burin Island into the open waters of Placentia Bay and began pitching into a big, slow, queasy swell running from the south. As *Happy Adventure* began to rise and sink with the rhythm of the swell I got out the bottle and made the customary offering to the Old Man of the Sea, then I passed a glass to Mike who was looking thoughtful.

Mike raised the glass to his lips, abruptly turned aside, and made his own personal offering to the Old Man. I do not think it was made voluntarily because Mike did not hold with pagan superstitions; but voluntary or not it was made with energy and with abandon.

When he was quite finished he turned palely to me and said he did not think he really cared for rounders – not twice on the same morning anyway.

The breeze freshened until we were bowling down the desolate Burin coast at a good five knots. Mike began to get the feel of things and to enjoy himself. I showed him how to steer a compass course. He had no trouble with the compass but he had some difficulty steering. This was because steering a boat by means of a tiller, instead of a wheel, requires the helmsman to push the tiller in the opposite direction to the way he wants the boat to turn. It takes a little while to get accustomed to it.

Before noon we rounded Lawn Head and altered course until we were running almost due west. The wind began to

fall light and the sky grew increasingly hazy. I kept one anxious eye to seaward, watching for the black wall of fog to start advancing, and the other on the grim, reef-strewn coast that we were skirting.

Mike, at his ease at the tiller, was more interested in the oceanic world and its inhabitants. He grew ecstatic when we passed through a pod of pothead whales, sleek black beasts fifteen feet or more in length, so busy pursuing schools of unseen squid that some of them surfaced and blew within a stone's throw of us.

Mike had recently re-read *Moby Dick* and he was fired by a desire to experience the passions of a whaler. I turned a deaf ear to his suggestion that he be allowed to put off in the dory, armed with our boat-hook, and harpoon a pothead for himself. Not that I was unsympathetic, but I was becoming increasingly worried about a spreading overcast and rapidly worsening visibility that was forcing us to hold ever closer to a most inhospitable coast.

My problem was that I could not simply take a course off the chart and steer by the compass, keeping a good offing from the land. The compass would not let me. Although we were then steering just south of west the compass insisted we were actually steering north-northwest. There was only one way we could navigate and that was by making use of landmarks on the shore; and landmarks on the shore of the Burin Peninsula are ill-defined at best.

About two o'clock I slung my binoculars around my neck and climbed to the foremast spreaders, hoping to pick up Lamaline Head, off which lies a formidable barrier of sunken rocks. Luck was with me and I was able to distinguish the distant Head. Feeling relatively secure for the moment I swung my binoculars in search of other vessels.

A mile off the port bow I saw something which resolved itself into an immense, glistening black back. I took it to be one of the great whales, either a finner or a blue. Since I too have long been fascinated by the great creatures of the sea, I called down to Mike telling him what I had seen and ordering him to alter course toward the beast.

As we ran down upon the animal Mike was as expectant as a child making his first visit to the zoo—and nearly as unmanageable. He kept letting go of the tiller in order to leap up on the cabin trunk for a better look, and it was only by bellowing like a Captain Queeg that I could keep him at his post at all. He grew even more excited when I called down to tell him it was not a whale—it was a shark; either a Greenland or a Basking shark, but in any event one of the largest true fishes in the sea.

It was immense. Lazing slowly on the surface with its dorsal fin standing up like a tri-sail, it appeared to be quite unconscious of our approach. This is a characteristic of both species for both are sluggish giants with, apparently, not much intelligence. Perhaps they don't need a great deal. This specimen was a good ten feet longer than our vessel and it was hard to imagine any natural antagonist that could threaten it.

Certainly I had no intention of threatening it, let alone attacking it. However I did want a close look so I told Mike to run alongside, keeping about thirty yards away.

Mike chose to interpret the distance as thirty feet and, as we drew abeam of it, the great fish, for some reason known only to itself, ponderously changed direction to cross our bows.

"Hard-a-starboard, Mike!" I yelled. "Hard over!"

In retrospect I can attach no blame to Mike. He had only just learned that starboard meant right. He had only just learned to steer a boat with a tiller. He *did* manage to remember which direction starboard was—and he hauled the *tiller* hard to starboard.

We were then travelling at about four knots, which is no great speed, but that shark was very nearly an immovable object and when we hit him, just behind the dorsal fin, we did so with a rubbery jolt that almost catapulted me off the foremast. *Happy Adventure*'s curving cutwater slipped up over his broad back until her bowsprit pointed skyward, then the monster sounded and the little ship sailed on.

Mike was all contrition but since as far as I could tell no harm had been done to anyone, I graciously forgave him. We sat and talked about the encounter. We were both much affected, for it is not often given to modern men to meet such a colossus from the alien sea world. Eventually I decided to go below and brew a pot of coffee.

When I stepped off the bottom of the companion ladder I stepped into several inches of cold water . . . .

Even in that first shocked moment I knew exactly what had happened. The collision with the shark had sprung a plank below the waterline. As I leapt for the pump I yelled at Mike to tell him we were holed; we were sinking! With vivid memories of the awful night spent outside Trepassey crowding in upon me I went at the pump with a sort of insane ferocity. Again! It had happened again! It was just too bloody much to bear!

Oh, how I pumped. Sweat filled my eyes. The pump itself grew warm to the touch. But I saw nothing, felt nothing, except a foul and consuming rage. I had no breath for words, but the oaths I mentally lavished on *Happy Adventure*, on Mike, on the Old Man, and even on St. Christopher, should have doomed me forever, even if the leak did not.

Then the pump sucked dry! The handle wobbled loosely in my hand.

I looked into the bilge opening beside the engine. The bilge was dry except for its usual coating of oily slime. There was no flood of cold green water pouring aft along the keelson.

I did not believe it. I stayed below watching the bilge for almost an hour and in that time the vessel took exactly as much water (it was quite enough, to be sure) as she usually took. There was no new leak.

Baffled but infinitely relieved I went back on deck and took over the helm and we resumed our voyage toward St. Pierre. I pondered the mystery of the flooded engine room but could form no idea of what might have happened.

After a time Mike went below to make the coffee. A few moments later he popped his head out through the companionway.

"Farley," he said, "there's no water in the fresh water pump. Can't get a drop."

Here was a new mystery. We had filled our fresh water tank before leaving Burin. It was an immense tank for so small a vessel, because Jack and I intended it to hold enough fresh water to last us clear across an ocean if need be. Now Mike insisted it was empty. Leaving *Happy Adventure* to look after herself I joined him down below, and in due course we found some answers.

The jolt when we hit the shark had caused an already slack hose connection on the bottom of the tank to shake free – and our entire supply of fresh water had flowed out into the bilges.

By the time we discovered what had happened we were well past Lamaline. Visibility had improved a little, and I was able to dimly distinguish a grey pimple on the far horizon and to recognize it for Colombier Island which lies close beside St. Pierre. I took the tiller again, having apologized to Mike, to *Happy Adventure*, to the shark, to St. Christopher, and to the Old Man of the Sea. Mike was discreetly busy down below. After a while he scrambled up on deck bearing two steaming mugs.

"Here, Skipper," he said. "Drink this. And begorra, I'll bet you've never tasted Irish coffee like it!"

In truth I never had. I probably never will again. But this I can confirm: black coffee made with rum as a substitute for water is a drink of exceptional authority.

At about six-thirty the wind fell out completely. By then we were within a few miles of the North Channel entry into St. Pierre, so we downed sail and started the bullgine for the final run. We made a triumphant approach. With a bone in her teeth and a pennant of black smoke trailing from her exhaust, the little ship drove in toward the grey, treeless loom of the French islands.

We passed a big rusty Portuguese freighter on her way out. Being full of the brotherhood of the sea we cheerfully saluted her with three feeble blasts on our hand fog-horn. After a short pause while her skipper tried to locate the source of the sound, for his vessel dwarfed us into insignificance, she responded with three mighty blasts. This was a proud moment – but it had repercussions.

The freighter had dropped the St. Pierre Pilot only a few minutes earlier, and the Pilot was on his way back to harbour in his big motor launch when he heard the whistle blast. He assumed that another vessel was preparing to enter and would require his services. As we swung around Ile aux Vainqueurs to enter the North Channel, we met the pilot boat coming back out.

She was twice our size and going twice as fast. Paying no attention to us she went racing past and then, seeing nothing on the horizon except the departing Portuguese freighter, began to circle in a puzzled sort of way. Finally she turned about and came foaming toward *Happy Adventure*.

When she was a few yards off she slowed and the Pilot hailed us in French, which left me little the wiser because my knowledge of that language is fragmentary. Mike spoke fluent French. To the Pilot's polite query as to whether we had seen another inbound vessel, Mike replied that indeed we had.

"Where is she?" asked the Pilot.

"Gone down!" Mike replied, pointing an expressive thumb towards the deeps.

"Gone down? Mon Dieu! You mean she sank?"

"Oui," said Mike affably. "But maybe submerged would be a better word. It was a submarine, Monsieur. A very big one. With a very big gun on the bow. It had a hammer and sickle painted in bright red on the conning tower."

The Pilot's face paled noticeably. His eyes rolled as he anxiously searched the horizon. I think he must have been about to flee for his life when some faint, lurking suspicion seemed to be aroused within him. His face began to redden. He turned back to us and saw the smirk upon Mike's face.

"By God, I think you are one big liar! Bien! The submarine is gone, but *you* remain. You wish to enter St. Pierre, eh? Then you will take a pilot. Stand by for me to come aboard."

This was the *only* part of the conversation Mike translated for me.

"Nothing doing," I said. "You tell him we don't need any pilot, aren't going to take one, and certainly aren't going to pay for one."

Mike passed this on, and the Pilot shrugged, grinned without mirth, jammed his engine into gear, and without more ado began describing circles around *Happy Adventure* at high speed, putting up a huge wake, and passing so close under our bow and stern that I could see his jaw muscles working each time he went by.

The little schooner was shocked by this behaviour and she showed it. She pranced; she leapt; she shook herself; she skated skittishly from side to side as each new wave hit her. As for me, I did not have a clue as to the cause of this outrageous behaviour on the part of the Pilot, and I was much annoyed by it. I was also still under the influence of the Irish coffee, which is a notably belligerent drink.

It so happened that as part of our lifesaving gear we carried a flare pistol of wartime vintage. I jumped below and got the gun. At the next pass the Pilot made I fired a flare two feet above his cabin roof! He sheered off so violently that he heeled his port gunwales under water. He did not return but ran at full throttle toward the harbour entrance and disappeared behind the mole.

That was undoubtedly one of the most satisfying exploits of my entire nautical career but, it has to be admitted, it was not necessarily the wisest. When, half an hour later, we puttered through the gap between the moles and opened the harbour itself, the first thing we saw was a platoon of gendarmes marshalling on the government wharf.

Mike claimed to be of the opinion that they had been called out to give us an official welcome. But the effect of the Irish coffee was wearing off and I was plagued with doubts. So instead of steaming boldly in and putting our lines ashore I stayed a hundred yards off the dock, coyly circling, while the gendarmes, the douanes, the immigration men, and a growing number of other citizens urgently beckoned us to come ashore.

At this point Mike drew my attention to two harbour launches, a small tug boat, and the pilot boat, all of which were busily embarking gendarmes. It appeared that if we were not anxious to go to them, they were anxious to come to us. I turned tail and *Happy Adventure* fled out through the

gap. I do not feel that we fled with ignominy. Being so considerably outnumbered, I doubt if even Nelson would have been willing to stand his ground.

The aftermath of that imbroglio might have been unpleasant had not luck been with us. As we galumphed slowly down the channel we met a large, seagoing dory, inward bound. Her name, *Oregon*, was written large across her bows and I recognized both her and the skipper. He was Théophile Detcheverry, descendant of generations of Basque fishermen who have lived on the islands during the last three hundred years. Théo was a great, bull-voiced, vibrant man; a power on the islands and also, thank the Lord, a friend of mine from a previous visit to St. Pierre.

Théo recognized me too. His bellow of welcome was perfectly audible above the roar of both our engines. He ran *Oregon* alongside of us with such abandon that *Happy Adventure* still bears the scars.

"Farleee! By Christ! You come back to St. Pierre at last! C'est bon! C'est magnifique! And in your own bateau, you come . . . !"

"Oui, Théophile," I said when I could get a word in edgewise. "I've come; but je ne pense pas that I'll be staying long. Regardez-vous astern!" With which I pointed to the pursuing flotilla rapidly closing in upon us.

At this point Mike took a hand. He explained the whole situation and when Théo got through laughing like a mad walrus he leapt aboard and instructed me to stop my engine. We were soon surrounded by the St. Pierre Home Defence Squadron and for a while all was pure pandemonium.

When things sorted themselves out we returned to the harbour with Théo at the tiller of *Happy Adventure*, with the rest of the fleet giving us a cheerful escort. It is a nice characteristic of the St. Pierrais that, although they are quick to flame, they are also quick to forgive.

They were very good about some other small matters to which I had forgotten to attend before we left Muddy Hole. For one thing, I had not obtained official clearance for my vessel to sail to foreign ports. Also, I had not bothered to have her registered and so I had no papers. No papers. No flag. No port of registration, and not even a name painted on her stern or bow. It was a wonder that Mike and I were not immediately jailed and our ship interned.

As soon as we moored, Théo came below accompanied by the Chef of the douane and one or two other uniformed officials. The Chef was a little sticky. He had a large hole in one of his teeth and he kept sucking at it in a pessimistic way while Théo insisted that, in our case, papers were not necessary. The Chef did not seem easy to convince. The four men argued long and hotly but to no avail until Théo had an inspiration. This is how he described it to us later.

"I told them, you see, that since your boat did not belong to any country it could be adopted. I reminded them that we were all of Basque ancestry, and that the Basques had once been the greatest seafaring people in the world but now, having been occupied by France and Spain, we did not have a single seagoing vessel sailing under our own flag. Why not, I asked them, adopt this good little boat? We will rechristen her. We will give her the flag of the Seven Basque Provinces. Yes, and we will give her a port of registry and papers all in *Basque*! And then there *will* be one ship upon the ocean flying the flag of our ancient Motherland! What could they say?"

What they said, of course, was yes; and they said it so enthusiastically that *I* never had any say in the matter at all. Which is how it came to pass that *Happy Adventure* ceased to be a Newfoundland vessel and became the flagship of the Basque mercantile marine.

13· *With soul so pure*

ONE MORNING before I am old and hoary I shall waken again to the sound of water slapping gently against the hull of a small vessel as she lies asleep beside the jetty in St. Pierre. I shall climb lazily out of my bunk, sniff the mingled smells of cod, coal smoke, and heather, then I shall amble across the wide Place bordering the harbour, to the Café L'Escal.

Madame Ella Girardin will see me coming and my croissants and coffee will be waiting on the bar. And if Ella detects a certain weakness in my gait there will be a small glass of brandy beside the coffee cup.

Some of the quiet fellows sitting at the little table will give me a casual "bonjour." Others may acknowledge my arrival with a greeting in Portuguese or Spanish. As I drink my breakfast I will listen to their comments on the state of the fishery and on the happenings in the world of ocean.

Morning is talking time, but eventually I shall go out on the cobbled streets that run uphill amongst the crowded narrow houses of the little town. If it is a sunny day I may go spearing lobsters at Ravenel Bay. Or I may hitch a ride in a dory with a friend of mine from Île aux Marins and go fifteen miles to sea to jig a cod or a haddock for tomorrow's lunch. Most likely, though, I'll amble down to the docks to have a gam with the sailors from one of the score or so of Portuguese, French, or Spanish draggers moored to the wharf.

In the afternoon I may make my way at a gentle pace up

the long, scrub-covered slopes behind the town and amble across the rough barrens, through blue lupins and strong-scented grass, to the high-domed crest of the rock ridge behind Cap au Diable. From there I'll look southeast over the neat reticule of the town; over the broad double harbour past Galantry Head to a far distant curl of foam bursting over the haunted reef that bears the name "Les Enfants Perdus," and beyond that to the shores of Canada—of Newfoundland.

After a while the fog will begin rolling in, and it will be time to descend the hill and walk through ghostly streets until I come to La Joinville, at whose long bar Jean will pour me a noggin, "to get the fog out of your bones," and tell me fantastic yarns of the great days of Le Whiskey when St. Pierre was the focal point of interest, and sometimes of guns as well, for the thirsting millions of a prohibition-smitten United States of America. Jean will tell me again how the rows of now gaunt and empty concrete warehouses along the waterfront were once stacked to their roof beams with hundreds of thousands of cases of whiskey, brandy, rum, and wines; and he will talk again of the elusive, hard-faced men who manned the swift and often nameless ships that came and went by night; sailing for dark rendezvous with black-painted motor boats off the coasts of the New England states.

I will do these things that I have done before; but there will be one thing I cannot do again. As evening draws down Théophile Detcheverry will not be there to welcome me into his rambling old house, and I will not be able to sit until the dawn hours watching the quick flow of passions on his saturnine and hawk-nosed face, while I listen to his great voice booming a mixture of good French and atrocious English, as he speaks of the islands he knew so well and loved so deeply. Théo is gone. But I will remember him, for it was he, more than any other man, who taught me to know the myth-shrouded little archipelago lying only twelve miles off the shores of Canada—the never-never land of St. Pierre and Miquelon.

Because the arrangements to make a Basque lady out of *Happy Adventure* would take several days, Théo suggested we should have the vessel hauled on the marine railway at the shipyard. He was sure the local shipwrights would be able to find and stanch her leaks, and while she was high and dry we would have time to repaint her and generally make her beautiful for her christening.

I was pessimistic about the chances of anyone *ever* stopping her leaks, but the mere prospect of not having to pump her for a day or two was so engaging that I set off at once to visit the shipyard and make the necessary arrangements.

The yard was decrepit, sprawling, and unbelievably cluttered. On one of its two slipways a Newfoundland schooner, the *Sandy Point*, stood high and dry, while the other slip was occupied by a sea-worn Spanish dragger. The whole place smelled of a mixture of old wood, sun-heated iron, stockholm tar, engine oil, and black, reeking coal smoke, coming from a ramshackle building that housed a massive and antique steam engine and winch, by means of which the ships were hauled up on the slips.

At the cradle holding the dragger, three or four workmen were hammering in big wooden wedges to hold her securely in position for a launching which, evidently, was due to take place at any moment.

A rotund, red-faced young man with a monk's fringe in lieu of hair emerged briefly from the steaming engine house, shouted something to the men preparing the dragger, and dashed back into his hissing inferno. I walked toward his lair and as I stepped over one of the launching rails I almost fell over a dog.

She was asleep. She lay on her back, legs outspread, with no pretence at modesty, her head turned at a painful angle, so that her nose rested on a pillow of scrap iron. She was big and black with a white chest; and she was snoring loudly.

As my foot came down within an inch of her face she opened one yellow eye and gave me a long, cold stare; but she continued to snore. The back hairs on my neck crawled a little as I hurried away from this monster who seemed able to observe the world with a watchful eye while she slept.

I had not gone three paces when the whistle atop the

engine house let loose a fearful shriek. The blast immobilized me but it galvanized the dog into frenetic action. She gained her feet with one leap and began to run with a loose-limbed gallop that carried her across the yard and out of sight into the maze of streets beyond.

The whistle ceased and the rotund cherub emerged again from his hotbox, wiping his brow with his shirt. He saw me and beckoned. The gesture was imperious.

"Allo, anyway!" he said as I approached. "I am Paulo. You like Napoleon?"

Napoleon is not one of my favourite figures from the past, but since this was French territory and I was an alien I equivocated.

"Je him aime beaucoup. Mais je pense De Gaulle is better!" I said carefully.

A faint shadow of bewilderment hovered over Paulo's rosy brow for a moment, then was gone.

"Eh, bien!" he cried. "Then drink!"

With which he shoved a bottle at me. It was Napoleon brandy. It was warm, but it was good.

Between drinks (for Paulo was not one of your single-drink men) I broached the subject of hauling out *Happy Adventure*.

"Pas de difficulté! We are enchanted. One hour after we launch this dragger, then we haul you out. But, Monsieur, why you do not have another drink?"

So I had another and then, because the effect of the encounter with the great black dog was still strong, I asked: "That chien, is it that she is yours? She acts like she is fou, crazy."

Paulo bellowed, a great gust of Napoleon-spiced mirth. "Crazee? That dog? That Blanche? Oh non, my fran. She is, what you say, more smart than me! You wait, you watch."

"Okay. Je watch. Mais why is it that you call her Blanche quand elle est noir as a lump de charbon?"

"Why not?" Paulo answered with some impatience. "How many people you know called Green, eh? Or Brown or Black?

What colour they are, eh? Anyhow, that dog, she has very pure soul. Sooo, Blanche, non?"

The logic seemed irrefutable. We sat together on a baulk of timber and waited. I assumed we were waiting for the men at the dragger cradle to signal they were ready for the launch. But when after a few minutes they shouted that all was in order, Paulo only beamed at them, waved the bottle, and went on sitting.

"Waitez vous to get up une gross tête de steam?" I asked.

"Non, non," said Paulo. "We wait for Blanche."

Then from around the town-side corner of the main ship-yard building appeared a bevy of wonderfully assorted dogs. There were five of them, and they ranged from a huge, pant-ing, lumbering, quasi-St. Bernard to a tiny, yapping, short-legged beast known in Newfoundland as a "crackie." They came around the corner fast. Bringing up the tail of the pro-cession was Blanche.

Paulo bounced to his feet and vanished into his inferno. He gave three short blasts on the whistle and the men at the dragger cradle jumped off. They had hardly cleared the cradle when dogs began scrambling aboard it. They showed little enthusiasm for what they were doing and one or two of them even made faint-hearted attempts to bolt back to-ward the town. It was useless. Like a black devil herding doomed souls into the nether pit, Blanche anticipated these attempts, and a snarl and a snap took the spirit of resistance out of the defectors.

The winch began to roar. The big drum began to turn and the cable to pay out. The cradle gave a jerk and began to slide down the slope toward the harbour. The dogs were silent except for the quasi-St. Bernard who closed his eyes and moaned hoarsely.

Soon all the dogs were afloat and milling aimlessly about in the froth. The cradle sank until only the tops of its arms were showing. The dragger started her engines and steamed out into the stream. The launch was over.

Well, it was not *quite* over. The harbour was now full of

floating objects. Many of these were hardwood wedges but five were the heads of swimming dogs. I now began to see a point and purpose in the strange scene I was witnessing.

Each dog swam to a wedge. Each dog, according to his or her size, ability, and strength, either grabbed hold of a wedge, or bunted one with its chest, and began laboriously dragging or pushing the heavy blocks toward shore.

Paulo emerged beside me, grinning widely.

"Not so crazee, eh? Blanche, she make all them damn dog work. Ils ne l'aiment pas, you bet, but by God, what can they do? They work, or they have bite. That Blanche, she boss them good."

Blanche was the last to regain the land. She shook herself, looked searchingly over the harbour to make sure there was nothing left to be retrieved and then, without so much as a glance at her assistants, walked sedately to her favourite sleeping-place and slumped into a relaxed position in the sun. Then, and only then, did the pack begin to slink away. They had been dismissed from duty.

I had a few questions to ask of Paulo. We adjourned to L'Escal and there he told me all.

Blanche, he explained, did not belong to him or, in fact, to any man. She hailed originally from the small outport of Grand Bruit, on the south shore of Newfoundland, a hundred miles west of St. Pierre.

Grand Bruit is famous for its black water dogs, which are not to be confused with either the kennel-bred Labrador or the giant Newfoundland breed. Both of these types were developed *from* the native water dog which seems to have evolved naturally in Newfoundland, or perhaps on St. Pierre, from a now vanished European species brought over by Basque fishermen hundreds of years ago. These dogs, whose aquatic prowess is truly phenomenal were, until recently, carried on almost every fishing vessel. They had a dual task: to act as lifesavers if a man fell overboard, and to retrieve codfish that escaped from the jigger as it was hauled to the surface.

For some years Blanche had gone fishing with her owner who was skipper of a little two-dory schooner out of Grand Bruit. Then one bitter February night this vessel went ashore on Galantry Head of St. Pierre. Her crew and dog made it safely to shore where they were cared for until the men could arrange a passage out.

The first passage that offered itself was aboard a big schooner belonging to Fortune Bay bound on a fishing voyage to the Grand Banks. Blanche's master left her in Paulo's care until he could return to claim her, but the schooner never returned to land. She went unreported, and no trace of her, or of her crew, was ever found.

Blanche made herself at home in the shipyard. Before her coming, the shipyard workers used to have to row about the harbour after a launching, in order to pick up the drifting wedges. But one morning Blanche decided to do the job for them. She did it so well that she went on the payroll of the yard.

Although she was very much a female she contemptuously rejected the advances of the scruffy mongrels of the town. They were not her type. Then one spring a handsome

black male of her own kind arrived aboard another New-foundland schooner. There was a whirlwind romance before her lover went back to sea – and Blanche was pregnant.

She stuck to her duties at the yard until Paulo and the other workers began to worry about her. It was not fitting, they felt, that a pregnant lady should work so hard and in such icy waters. They tried to persuade her to take a leave of absence but Blanche refused. She had her own solution to the problem.

One afternoon when she was about four weeks gone and Paulo signalled for a launch, instead of racing to the cradle Blanche shot out of the yard and disappeared. Paulo was surprised, but he was much more surprised when, a few minutes later, she reappeared nipping at the heels of a large spaniel belonging to the Governor of St. Pierre.

Relentlessly she chivvied this poor beast down to the cradle, drove him aboard, and kept him there while the launch was made. Whereupon she forced him to help collect the wedges.

"She train that dog just once," Paulo explained, "and after that, he know what he have to do. He don't like it. Mon Dieu, he scream like hell first time, but he have no choice. Afterward, when I blow the whistle, Blanche she go and get him. One time he go away and hide, but next day she catch him on the street and tear one ear mostly off his head. After that he do what he is told."

Before her pups were born, Blanche had expanded her task force and trained them so well that they could do the job entirely on their own. After her pups were weaned and had gone to sea on various ships, she maintained her shore crew, not because she really needed them but, it must be assumed, for the pleasure of making honest working dogs out of a bunch of "townee" loafers.

"Every now and again she break in a new one," Paulo continued. "That Doberman, he is a new one. Very bad swimmer too. I hope he don't drown. He belong to the new Chef des Gendarmes, another damn Frenchman from Paree . . . ."

That same afternoon *Happy Adventure* went on the cradle the dragger had occupied and was whisked ashore. She seemed like a toy boat in the midst of all that machinery, dwarfed into insignificance by the *Sandy Point* on the adjoining slip.

As Mike inelegantly put it, "Looks like the *Sandy Point* gave birth to a green preemy. Wonder if it'll live?"

Indeed *Happy Adventure* seemed a sickly child. Not only was her colour awful, but her general state of health left a great deal to be desired. When the caulking crew gathered to examine her dripping bottom there was much clucking and head-shaking and expressive eye-rolling.

Nevertheless they went to work on her and they worked with a will. Unbelievable quantities of caulking cotton vanished into her gaping seams. One entire plank, so rotten that a man could shove his knife right through it, was removed and replaced. All of her stopwaters were drilled out and new ones installed; and a number of other ailments were attended to.

Mike and I had received specific instructions from Théo about repainting her.

"You will please, Messieurs, remove that green!" he told us. "Her hull, she will be black. Her boot top, she will be white. Her bottom, she will be red. Below her rail, you will please to paint a yellow line. Her decks, they will be dory-buff. Her masts, you will scrape and then you will oil, and you will paint the trucks white. When you have finished she will not look like something very dead pulled out of the sea, she will look like a fine Basque ship!"

During the next few days preparations for the christening were being completed. These were under the management of Théo's son-in-law, Martin Dutin, who became Chef de Protocol for the event.

Martin's tasks included making arrangements for a Dominican Father to give the vessel a formal baptism; the manufacture of a Basque flag to be flown at our masthead; the philological problem of translating the words *Happy Adventure* into the Basque language; plans for the public christen-

ing ceremony; and finally arrangements for a mighty party to celebrate the rebirth of the Basque mercantile marine.

Our launching was something of a celebration in its own right. While Blanche gathered her minions on the cradle, most of the shipyard workers and a number of Spanish sailors crowded aboard, laden with launching gifts, mostly of a liquid nature. The cradle descended smoothly and *Happy Adventure* floated again. Many willing hands fumblingly untied the lines that held her fast. She drifted clear of the cradle and of the busy dogs. Mike started the bullgine and we motored to a berth at the main government wharf. It had been a good launching and the ministrations of the shipyard people seemed to have cured *Happy Adventure*'s leakiness. This was cause for further celebration so we all adjourned to the Café L'Escal.

Mike and I left L'Escal very late that dark and foggy night.

We had neglected to bring a flashlight with us, so our only source of illumination was the inner glow that suffused us both. We had the devil's own time finding the harbour. When we did find it we had no idea at what point on its perimeter we had arrived. We spent an hour groping our way along the seawall, painfully locating the mooring wires of draggers with our shins.

Of *Happy Adventure* we could find neither hide nor hair. I concluded we should give up the search and go back to L'Escal, wake Ella up and ask her for a bed. However Mike was in the grip of a stubborn Irish streak, than which there is no stubborner. Muttering to himself, he dragged me with him until we encountered yet another mooring wire.

It was not *Happy Adventure*'s warp. It led instead to the slimy deck of a truly antediluvian schooner that, for as long as anyone could remember, had lain beside a remote portion of the harbour wall.

Years and years earlier this schooner, the *Diamant*, had given up her tenuous hold on life and had partly sunk at her moorings. But down in her mildewed cabin there lived a mariner as ancient as the ship. He was only seen on rare occasions, when he popped out of the vessel's afterhatch to scuttle rapidly across the Place to one of the more disreputable bars.

Having found something he recognized, Mike was encouraged to crawl cautiously aboard. He was determined to wake up the old man of the *Diamant* and ask him if *he* knew anything concerning the whereabouts of our vessel.

The hatch slid back and out popped the head of the resident gnome, his grizzled and shrunken face glowing in the light of an oil lantern. He seemed to know what we wanted. Waving the lantern he beckoned us to follow him over the outer rail on to the deck of a moribund, wooden motor launch, belonging to our good friend Paulo. Moored snuggly alongside Paulo's boat was our missing ship.

The arrival of two fog-belated foreign draggers at the crowded wharf had occasioned *Happy Adventure*'s removal to this new location, but the sailors who moved her had not felt it necessary to inform us of their action.

Our guide departed, taking his lantern – leaving us to fumble our way aboard our ship, and to descend into the black depths of *Happy Adventure*'s interior without even the flare of a match to light the way.

I was by now so well used to her and had had so many intimate contacts with deck beams, protruding engine parts, and other obstacles, that I could avoid them blindfolded. So I went below first – and immediately came to grief. I put my foot through something that crunched, went sprawling, and ended up embracing the cold torso of the engine.

I did not swear because I was scared half out of my wits. I was not alone in the engine room. All around me was a scaly, whispering, scratching sound, and things were moving under my prone body and crawling over my spread legs. I scrabbled clear, found the lamp in the main cabin, and with trembling hands managed to light it. Mike started down the companion ladder, and stopped. In the soft lamplight both of us could see *why* we were not alone.

Earlier that evening Paulo had brought us a present. It was a large cardboard carton filled to the top with crabs. Finding nobody at home he had placed the carton at the foot of the companion ladder where we would be sure to find it.

These were not your little, insignificant, beach crabs; they were large, robust, and active deep-water crabs with a shell span of six inches or more and formidable pincers. There were dozens of them. Paulo had intended us to have a mighty feast but the crabs thought otherwise. We managed to corral a few and put them in a pail, but the rest proved too elusive, or too well-armed, for us to cope with. Most of them made it into the security of the bilges where they disappeared under the floor boards.

Having assured each other that, unlike the palm-tree crabs of the Pacific, St. Pierre crabs could not climb, we rolled wearily into our bunks intending to take up the pursuit on the morrow; in daylight and wearing rubber boots.

It had been a long, exhausting day.

14. Itchy-Ass-Sally

MIKE AND I and the crabs went to sleep at about four o'clock as a heavy rain began to hammer on the top of the cabin. We were awakened at seven by a heavy hand hammering on the top of the cabin.

In no good humour I slid back the hatch and found that it was still raining and that the fog was as thick as ever. Standing on the deck of Paulo's boat was a bedraggled group of people consisting of a young priest, two small boys whom I took to be his acolytes, Théophile Detcheverry, his son George, and Martin Dutin. In that eerie dawn light they looked like a Dürer print of mourners come to claim a corpse.

In fact they had come to conduct the official baptism service over *Happy Adventure*; to wash away her Protestant sins as it were, and make an honest woman of her.

As they crowded into the narrow confines of the untidy cabin Martin whispered apologies for the earliness of the visit, explaining that this was the only free time the Father had been able to find. He added that the Father had a tearing head cold, could hardly talk, and wished to get the job over in a hurry.

I had no objections. It was distinctly chilly standing there in my underwear and I longed to be back in my warm sleeping-bag. Mike, who was not even wearing underwear, was still in his bag and showed no inclination to leave it.

The service was mercifully simple. While the two little boys intoned a chant, the Father produced a bottle of holy water, uncorked it, and poised it directly over our saloon table.

With the exception of Mike we all tried to stand erect, which cannot be done in *Happy Adventure*'s cabin. Our heads were bowed, perforce, and so were our legs and our backs. As for Mike, he squirmed about until he managed to get into a semi-kneeling position, still inside his sleeping-bag, but he did not look particularly reverent. He looked more like a dissipated camel-driver waking at dawn in the bitter cold of the desert to have a morning chat with Mohammed.

Snuffling gently, the Father said a prayer or two and then prepared to give the little vessel her new name. At the precise moment that he pronounced it and tipped the bottle, he was convulsed by a gargantuan sneeze.

Holy water flew everywhere. A glittering parabola curved across the table and landed on Mike's bunk. Ricochet droplets spattered the intent faces of the rest of us. Fearfully embarrassed, the Father hurriedly mumbled the rest of the blessing and beat a hasty retreat.

The Detcheverrys and Martin also departed and Mike and I and the crabs were left alone to meditate on what had taken place. Mike's sympathy for the unfortunate Father was a little deeper than mine.

"Don't you snigger, Mowat!" he said as he wiped holy water off his sleeping-bag. "You try saying the name of this silly damn boat and see what happens!"

I tried, and I saw what he meant. But why don't you, dear reader, try it for yourself?

Itchatchozale Alai.

Although Mike and I spent some time practising the name, we did not master it successfully, then or ever. Mike eventually produced a modified version which seemed to delight him, but which I felt – on behalf of my little ship – was not *really* acceptable.

Itchy-ass-sally did not seem quite the thing.

Newfoundlanders have a saying that a voyage badly begun will come to a good conclusion. It was so with our christening. While we were still struggling with the new name, Théo and Martin returned aboard bearing a bottle of a peculiar green liquid.

Heedless of the rain Théo climbed into our tiny dory and began painting the vessel's new name in gold on both bows. Meantime, Martin proudly displayed the new flag which had been made for us – a gorgeous confection of silk embroidered with gold thread. Emblazoned on its red background was a green-and-white cross and the crest of the seven provinces; those that formed the Basque nation before the French seized four of them and the Spaniards seized the other three.

Having formally presented me with the flag Martin opened the bottle of green liquor. "This," he told us, "is Izaro. It is the national drink of the Basque nation. Now we will toast *Itchatchozale Alai* in her native brew!"

We did so and immediately thereafter the day began to brighten. Having sampled Izaro, I no longer wondered why it took the Spanish and French eight hundred years to overrun the Basques; and I understood why, to this day, they have not yet succeeded in subduing them.

By eleven o'clock, the hour set for the public christening, the rain had stopped and the fog had thinned. A large crowd had gathered on the wharf and a number of specially invited guests had assembled on Paulo's boat.

The captain and crew of one Spanish Basque dragger had risked the terrors of Franco's vengeance by resolutely dressing all of their rusty vessel with every flag and pennant they could find.

Paulo had "borrowed" a brass cannon of ancient vintage from the front lawn of the governor's house, and had mounted it on the bow of his old boat, where he and a chum were busy doing things with a can of black powder and wads of cotton.

Precisely on the hour Martin, as Chef de Protocol, mounted to the top of the cabin of Paulo's boat. The local Basque musical group, clad in traditional costumes, sounded a fanfare. Martin made a charming little speech in French and in Basque. When he finished he turned to Madame Detcheverry, who had been chosen to be godmother to the vessel, and invited her to do her duty.

She did it with a will, swinging a ribbon-tethered bottle of Izaro with such enthusiasm that the bottle missed the vessel's bows, snapped its ribbon, soared up over our decks, and shattered against the mainmast ten feet above our heads. Then St. Pierre paid tribute to our little ship. Vessel horns and sirens sounded and reverberated across the harbour. And, somewhat delayed because of trouble with his quickmatch, Paulo fired his cannon.

This was a master-stroke. The heavy brass tube spouted a five-foot tongue of flame through an immense cloud of black smoke, letting loose a roar like that of worlds in collision. Luckily nobody was standing behind the gun. It snapped the ropes Paulo had used to bind it to his winch, shot backward like a rocket, smashed through the front of his wheel-house, and came out the other side, where it lay on the afterdeck, smoking gently, exhausted by its effort.

For the balance of the day *Itchatchozale Alai* was hostess to innumerable well-wishers; and that evening Ella Girardin gave a gala reception in the vessel's honour at L'Escal.

The party had two major results. One was that we decided to sail *Itchy* (this diminutive was bestowed on her that night when even the Basque speakers began having trouble pronouncing her name) on a ceremonial voyage to the Basque stronghold of Miquelon. The other was the signing on of a new crew member in the person of a golden-haired young fugitive from Toronto by the name of Claire, who had come to spend a month on the islands in order to perfect her command of the French language. It was not long before I persuaded her to include in her studies a course in advanced English, with myself as her instructor.

Resplendent in her new coat of paint; her name flashing in letters of gold; her new flag flying gaily from atop the mainmast; her compass adjusted and her engine temporarily amenable to reason, *Itchy* looked and acted like a new ship. I felt myself becoming discreetly proud of her and I even felt some modest confidence in her as well. It was in such a mood that we prepared to sail for Miquelon three days after the christening.

The assembled guests for the voyage numbered fifteen people and two dogs. The guests were accompanied by an incredible assortment of paraphernalia including sporting guns, huge hampers of food and huger hampers of wine and spirits, a telescope, several deck-chairs, and a spring-operated Victrola.

We attempted to find space for everything and everybody and we failed. There simply was not that much room. The indefatigable Martin thereupon dashed off down the harbour wall. He returned ten minutes later at the oars of a dory that was nearly as long as *Itchy*. We made this monster fast to our stern and filled it with "expendables," including the dogs, the deck-chairs, and three of the less attractive ladies. None of these three unfortunates had ever been in a boat before, so they accepted my assurances that they were being allowed to occupy what amounted to deluxe accommodations, leaving the rest of us to endure steerage conditions aboard the crowded schooner.

Our departure was not dashing. The unwieldy dory towing astern did not add to *Itchy*'s nimbleness. Even with the engine bellowing at full throttle and all sails set and drawing, we crawled out of the harbour at a speed of less than three knots.

The voyage was generally uneventful, but there were some minor incidents. As we were crossing the great bight between Langlade and Miquelon the tow-line parted and the dory went adrift. Rescue operations were not undertaken immediately because some of our crew, noting how *Itchy*'s speed and performance were improved by the loss of the dory, concluded that the dory passengers should be left to row to Miquelon in their own time. This proposition was finally rejected on humane grounds. Most of us felt it would be un-

fair to expose the two dogs to the privations of having to spend a night at sea.

There was a further incident when two of our most charming ladies went below to unpack the food hamper (the liquor hampers had already unpacked themselves). Both ladies quickly reappeared and were very, very sick, mostly overboard but quite a lot over themselves and over those who were crowded into the cockpit.

When they had partly recovered they rebuked Mike and me with baleful words. They said the stink in the cabin was enough to make a dead horse vomit. However, being French, they were prone to overstatement. The smell was not that bad. In fact Mike and I had learned to live with it and did not really notice it any more. It came from the several dozen crabs who had crawled up under the floorboards and there, poisoned by the bilge water, had gone to their eternal rest in places from which it was quite impossible to retrieve their mortal remains.

The presence of the crabs resulted in a piquant tableau. One of our guests was so overcome at finding himself afloat in such a small shallop on such a mighty ocean that he could not remain on deck. However, because of the crabs, he could not remain below either. He resolved this dilemma by spending the entire voyage crouched in the cabin with his head thrust out through a porthole. Seen from on deck, he looked like a stuffed moosehead that had shed its horns.

After eight or nine hours at sea we entered the wide, shingle-rimmed expanse of Miquelon Roads just at dusk. News of our coming had gone before us and, as we rounded Chat Rock and opened the mighty sweep of the beach, a dozen big, steeply sheered, multi-coloured Miquelon dories (each with a small deckhouse amidship which gave them an oddly Venetian look) were launched from their rollers and came out to meet us.

The settlement at Miquelon is almost wholly Basque and its people received *Itchy* as if she was truly one of their own, come home at last from over the shadowed seas of time. The dories formed an escort around us, and we bore down upon the attenuated little village with our Basque flag snapping proudly overhead.

Surrounded by an ebullient mass of people we straggled up to the village—the Bourg de Miquelon—past the grey, looming church, to the sandy track that was the only street. At night this street became a dormitory for many small black ponies and many large black dogs. They sprawled every which way across the track and, being black, were not readily distinguishable one from the other.

Later that night Mike was making his way along the track when he stumbled over a sleeping beast. Being a polite fellow he tried to make amends.

"Good doggie. Nice doggie. Nice old chap!" he said placatingly.

The dog replied with a shrill, vindictive whinny and Mike

was so startled he stumbled backward to collide with yet another sleeping form. He was not about to make another mistake in identification.

"Sorry, horsie!" he said hurriedly as he staggered clear.

I met him a few minutes later and he was confused.

"Listen!" he muttered uneasily. "I think we should get the hell out of here. It's bad enough to be whinnied at by a goddamn dog but when the horses start growling at you it's time to leave!"

Basque hospitality turned out to be everything we had been led to expect. By midnight all formalities had vanished in potent solvents and there was so much gaiety that the dogs and horses could no longer sleep. They went moodily off to the football field to spend the night, but I went back to my vessel.

A little breeze had sprung up from easterly and although it was only a zephyr I was uneasy about *Itchy*'s moorings. I made myself a pot of coffee and sat on deck, sniffing at the arriving fog and listening to the slow surge of the long ocean swells sucking against the pilings of the wharf. Slowly I became aware of a new noise coming off the unseen sea. It was a muffled throbbing; a slow heartbeat, which is the inimitable and unmistakable sound of a make-and-break engine. Somebody was making a belated entry into Miquelon Roads in a small boat. I hoped they knew where they were going because by then it was impossible to see more than a few yards.

A few minutes later the sound of the engine died into silence. There was a swish of parting waters at a boat's bow and something bumped gently alongside *Itchy*'s hull.

"Ahoy there, throw up your painter and I'll make you fast!" I called into the darkness.

There was continuing silence for a moment, a silence vaguely disturbed by deep and sibilant breathing, then a hoarse voice quavered:

"Who be ye?"

"*Itchatchozale Alai*, out of St. Pierre."

"Lard Jasus, bye, we's glad to hear it! We t'ought you was

the cutter waitin' to take we. We t'ought we was condemned!"

Somebody tossed me a line. I made it fast and two oilskin-clad figures clambered onto *Itchy*'s deck. They introduced themselves as the Manuel brothers.

There was Almon and there was Hondas. Almon, the elder, was in his late forties; a broad-bowed, square-built man with a seamed red face and wild blue eyes. Hondas, a year or two younger, was even more heavily built, but dark of hair and eye and skin. They were, however, alike in the way they smiled, not only at everything one said to them, but at everything *they* said in return. They were a merry pair.

They were also a greatly relieved pair, as I discovered when they followed me below to warm themselves with rum and coffee. They told me they were inward bound from Selbys Cove in Hermitage Bay on the Newfoundland coast, forty miles to the north of Miquelon.

"We's come for a drop o' stuff, ye know," Almon explained. "And me dear man, when we come alongside o' you, we was sure and believed 'twas the Mounties waiting for we. A hard crowd, they are too!" For once his smile faded a little.

"Aye," Hondas put in, "'twould have meant hard times in Selbys Cove if they'd a took we, wit' t'ree weddings comin' up next week and nary a drop to drink!"

After the Manuels had had their "warm" I accompanied them up to the village to meet their merchant, a local fisherman who also ran a small "export business", and who welcomed the Manuels hugely. Having been assured by all hands that the wind would not get any stronger, I was persuaded to sit with the three men in the kitchen while they talked about the "game."

More than a hundred and forty years ago the British government, acting on behalf of the predacious merchants of St. John's, decided to stop free trade between the scattered and isolated fishing outports of Newfoundland's south coast, and St. Pierre and Miquelon. And so began a struggle that continues to this day. The authorities refer to it as the war against smuggling; the people concerned refer to it simply as the "game."

For seven or eight generations boats have been putting out on foggy nights from tiny coves of Newfoundland's coast to feel their way in blackness over the uneasy seas to Miquelon or to St. Pierre. In the old days they traded fish bait, salmon, firewood, caribou meat, and furs, for sugar, flour clothing, tea, and rum.

In recent years the pattern has changed. There is no longer a shortage of staples in southern Newfoundland but the shortage of alcohol remains as acute as ever it was. The night-time customers who come to Miquelon now pay cash, not for rum, but for pure grain alcohol. Alky, as it is called, is supplied tax-free in five-litre cans (two cans packed in a wooden case), or in twenty-litre metal drums at a cost of about fifty cents a litre. A litre, properly diluted with water, is the equivalent in potency of three or four quarts of legal booze.

Until Confederation with Canada, the Newfoundland government's preventive force consisted of a number of old revenue cutters manned by native Newfoundlanders whose sympathies lay with the fishermen. In those days few arrests were made. However after Confederation the prevention duties were handed over to the Royal Canadian Mounted Police, a notoriously efficient and unsympathetic organization.

The R.C.M.P. set out in earnest to kill the game, bringing into use fast motor vessels, such as the *Commissioner Wood*, a real gunboat, half as big as a destroyer, manned by twenty or thirty policemen and fitted with quick-firing cannon, radar, special radios, and a host of modern aids in the preservation of law and order. By all realistic calculations, the R.C.M.P.—the Mounties—should have been able to win the game hands down. That they did not do so, and have not yet done so, is a proper tribute to the independence, intelligence, skill, hardihood, and thirst of the fishermen of southern Newfoundland.

When the Manuel brothers returned to their skiff I went

with them to help load their cargo. It consisted of six crates of alcohol – twelve cans in all. As we were heaving the crates aboard I noticed there were a number of large sacks of something in the fish hold.

As each crate came over the rail Hondas attached a line to it, and at the other end of the line tied one of the sacks. These sacks were filled with salt. The salt had been supplied free, as a fisherman's subsidy, by the unwitting Canadian government – a delicious touch of humour. The Manuels explained to me that this salt was their "insurance."

"If one o' they cutters comes onto we, we heaves bags and boxes over side. The salt, bein' heavy, takes the boxes straight down below, and there they stays 'till the salt melts into the water. How long that'll take depends on how much salt you uses and what kind o' bag. A brin bag'll soak out fifty pounds o' salt in fifteen hours; but fifty pounds in a flour sack'll take nigh onto twenty-four hours. You can time it pretty close, you know. And when 'tis time for the crates to come afloat why there'll be a couple o' dories nearby, jiggin' for cod as innocent as you please. The dorymen puts the cases into their holds, covers 'em up with cod, and that's an end of it, and the Mounties not a whit the wiser."

The Manuels found a sympathetic listener in me, for I am in favour of anything that takes the mickey out of duly constituted authority, whenever that authority intrudes on the freedom of the individual. I am also in favour of inexpensive booze.

When the loading was completed Almon gave me a long speculative look. He was making up his mind about something. Finally he spoke.

"Skipper," he said slowly, " 'tis a fine little vessel you've got. I wouldn't doubt she'd carry a fair cargo. What would ye say to a little voyage down into Hermitage Bay?"

I hesitated for a good tenth of a second. "I'd say yes."

We shook hands all around and had a final tot. The Manuels climbed aboard their cockle-shell and the overloaded skiff puttered off into the embracing blackness of fog and night.

The Manuels' invitation was not destined to be accepted immediately. On our return voyage from Miquelon to St. Pierre the next day, the bullgine ran out of goodwill and reverted to her usual bestial nature. She could be made to go only if I squatted over her whirling flywheel with one finger pressed against the igniter rod. This rod was hot. The fumes from the engine were suffocating. And the posture I had to maintain, in order to avoid being emasculated by the fly-wheel, was so crippling that it was some hours after we reached St. Pierre before I could stand upright.

That night, after our guests had departed, I made a solemn vow that *Itchy* would not sail again until the bullgine had been brought to heel once and for all. There would be too much at stake to allow us to take risks when she made her next voyage.

15 *Voyage of the* Oregon

I took the problem of the bullgine to Paulo who arranged for St. Pierre's most talented mechanic to deal with it.

This man, Jean-Pierre, a squat, black-bearded fellow who wore a greasy beret pulled down over his ears like a helmet could make or fix almost anything. During the war years he made an airplane with which to defend his home islands in the event that the Luftwaffe dared to threaten them. On its maiden flight from a pasture south of the town it hit a passing cow and, although the cow was killed, Jean-Pierre was uninjured. "Très fort! Cet aéroplane!" he told me with the pride of a good workman.

Jean-Pierre thought it would take three days to rebuild the bullgine, and on one of those days Théophile invited Claire and me to take a trip in his great dory, *Oregon*.

Théo's dory did not derive her name from a state in the American union but from a ship. The orginal *Oregon* was a big passenger liner. During the war while she was making a passage from Europe to Halifax laden with refugees (most of whom were women and children), she had engine trouble and fell behind the rest of her convoy.

She was then not far off the French islands and so her captain decided to put into St. Pierre for repairs. He had never been there before and his charts were not up-to-date. Because of the war the lighthouses and fog-horns were not functioning. Nevertheless *Oregon*'s master attempted to enter the North Channel in darkness and in fog; without radar and without a pilot.

That same night Théo was returning in his dory from a trip to Miquelon, feeling his own way through the fog by means of the special senses which he and his race had long since perfected. He heard the steamer before he saw her and changed course to see what manner of ship was attempting the entry channel on such a night.

She loomed up suddenly ahead of him, a monstrous black shape that he at first took to be a German warship, the *Scharnhorst*, making a raid upon the islands. However as he swung along her cliff-like side he realized that she was a passenger vessel.

He also realized that she was in desperate danger. She was proceeding directly toward St. Pierre Rock which lay in mid-channel less than half a mile ahead of her.

It is not easy for a man in a small boat, in almost total darkness, and without lights, to attract the attention of bridge officers on a big ship. Théo did it. He afterwards claimed it cost him his voice, although anyone who has heard his bass bellow will not take that claim too seriously. In any event he did make himself heard and persuaded the captain to stop the ship. He then boarded the big vessel, backed her clear of danger, and piloted her into the harbour.

Théo refused to accept a reward for saving the ship and, in all probability, the lives of many of her passengers. He asked only that he be permitted to name his dory after the vessel in memory of the event.

Ostensibly, the voyage on which Claire and I had been invited was intended to carry Martin Dutin, a young teacher named Bernard, and their wives to the Grand Barachois of Miquelon, where they were to spend a few days hunting and fishing. But for Claire and for me it was to be a holiday cruise, during which we would explore some of those places along the island coasts that were particularly dear to Théo and which he wished to share with us. Poor Mike was left behind as *Itchy*'s chaperone.

Very early on a sunny morning Claire and I made our way to the Hard where *Oregon* lay waiting. The dory was high and dry on the beach, enveloped in the now familiar stench of rotting cod livers. Twenty-five feet long, flat bottomed, and completely open, she looked awkward and ungainly as she lay upon the land.

We found the rest of the party already assembled, accompanied by the usual hampers of good things to eat and drink. Théo greeted us wearing a boiler suit and a tropical pith helmet. Théo was a man of many heroes and he not infrequently imitated them in dress. This day he was honouring a rather ill-assorted couple: Winston Churchill and Field Marshal Rommel.

The capstan was slacked off and *Oregon* slid heavily down wooden rollers into the sea. We set course out of the harbour on still waters under the unfamiliar benison of a rising sun. Wisps of mist still clung to the highlands but there was no fog to hide the world from our view. The ladies made themselves comfortable under rugs up in the bows and we gentlemen congregated aft around the big tiller – and passed the bottle.

Amidship, a four-horsepower version of my bullgine muttered and stuttered. Théo's knowing hand was never far from it, for it was as temperamental as all its kin. Théo had kept it running for more than thirty years, having inherited it from *his* father. It was a mass of brazing, welding, soldering, and grafted parts, but still it ran, after its fashion. It drove the four-ton bulk of *Oregon* along at a good pace, so that she went hissing and plunging over the ever-present swell, with the lift and liveliness of a Viking longship.

Leaving the North Channel we turned under the monumental loom of Grand Colombier, a mere dot of an island that rises sheer from the sea to a height of more than six hundred feet. Flocks of puffins wheeled away from the cliff-faces as we approached, and a blood-red light was reflected in the swirling waters from the ruddy rocks. It was a forbidding yet fascinating sight, and Bernard and I determined to land and scale the heights.

I am sure nobody but Théo could have put *Oregon* alongside those cliffs in the heaving, foaming surge that fringed them. With consummate skill he somehow managed it. As the dory swept in upon a surge we leapt from the bows to the slimy rock. Théo immediately reversed the engine and the dory drew safely clear again.

It was a long, hard climb, made particularly memorable by the fact that the cliff was riddled with abandoned puffin burrows, interspersed with other holes in which there lived a myriad of large, brown rats. Originally the island had belonged solely to the puffins, but years ago a ship was wrecked upon it and the only survivors were some rats. They made themselves at home and eventually established a symbiotic relationship with the puffins. According to Théo the rats survived mainly by eating dead puffins, puffin guano, young puffins in season, and unhatched puffin eggs. The puffins, for their part, discovered they could reduce the necessity of making long and tedious trips to sea each morning to fish for food, by entering the rats' burrows and feeding on baby rats.

The puffins had finished breeding when we were there but the rats were at home in numbers. They did not seem to like us much, nor did they fear us, and several times I found my-

self staring eyeball to eyeball at a large rat that seemed prepared to defend its territory by force.

Gaining the crest we discovered one of the oddest little worlds I have ever seen. The top of Colombier was a flat plateau, three or four acres in extent, surrounded by a rim of rock ten or fifteen feet in height. A lush growth of mosses, lichens, small bushes, and flowering plants carpeted the enclosed space, in the centre of which lay a small, ultramarine-tinted pond. Berries grew all about in great profusion.

When I mounted the natural rock palisade surrounding and protecting this minute paradise, I looked across the intervening straits to see the islands of St. Pierre and Langlade looming like truncated mountains, standing up to their shoulders in green waters. Those waters were so far below me that I mistook a passing dory for the fin of a great shark. The sky was an ephemeral blue but there was a misty flame in the east, producing an antediluvian effect, as of colossal images set in the midst of a dead sea.

We descended again through the cliff dwellings of the indignant rats and leapt aboard the waiting dory. *Oregon* crossed the wide channel called La Baie without difficulty although through it there runs a murderous tide rip. We then came under the massive lee of the cliffs of Langlade. Passing the bottle and lifting our faces to the warmth of the rising sun, we puttered along under the corrugated face of the big island until we reached Cap Percé and Percé Rock. Percé Rock is a bastion flung out by the high cliffs, and pierced by a tunnel, through which the dory stuttered in an echoing passage that sent a flight of resting stormy petrels flitting away like monster butterflies.

We moved on to Anse aux Soldats, where there was a tiny pebble beach sternly circumscribed by sea cliffs, on which lived two families who made their year's livelihood during the few brief days of the annual capelin run.

To this minute strip of beach the mysterious small fishes called capelin come in early July in erotic millions. They ride the waves high up on the beach; gleaming green males and less flamboyant females, side by side. As the wave withdraws they lie in a glittering and living carpet, shimmering in ecstasy as the females discharge their eggs and the males their milt. With the next wave they wash back into the dark sea.

During the brief period of the run the little fishes are shovelled up in immense numbers and spread to dry in the sun on the beach stones and on wire racks. Tons of the dried fishes are shipped to France where they are sold as a delicacy. When toasted and eaten whole, accompanied by good red wine, they are a gourmet's dream.

The capelin fishers, a jovial lot, came down to welcome us and there was much badinage and laughter from strong men and stout women. There was also one small boy who had put to sea to greet us in a miniature dory no bigger than a bathtub. In this pumpkin seed he dared the surging surf to fish for lobsters amongst the very claws of the sea cliffs.

We would have been content to linger here, but our safari leader hurried us back to *Oregon* and on we went, passing the ominous bulk of Cap aux Morts, and bringing into view a vast bight, at whose far horizon the sun reflected a thread-like ribbon of saffron light from La Dune – a seven-mile-long isthmus of sand that tenuously connects Langlade with Great Miquelon.

That curving yellow scimitar was only just visible on this, a clear white day without a trace of fog. It was easy to understand why it became a dreaded killer of men and ships on days when the fog drew down; or on black nights, when the great winds send the driving seas streaming in driven spume across the hidden shoals. No one knows with any certainty how many ships La Dune has killed, but there is a map extant that charts the burial places of more than a hundred vessels that were betrayed onto this strand of death. Their bones litter its empty beaches still.

Our destination, the Grand Barachois, is a vast salt-water lagoon embraced within the hour-glass base of the isthmus where it connects with mountainous Miquelon. The narrow entrance to the Barachois is impassable except at the turn of the tide by reason of the fierce currents that sweep in and out of it – so we had to wait a while. It was a pleasant wait. We beached *Oregon* midway along the isthmus on the gleaming sands and went exploring.

Flocks of plover scampered in front of us where immense jellyfish, purple and gold, fringed the waterline. Beyond the shore the dunes lifted and rolled, devoid of life except for stunted clumps of sand grass and a herd of little horses long gone wild, that threw up their heads at us, snorted fiercely, and went streaming off into the hazed distance.

There was little life, but there was much evidence of death. Within an hour we counted the remains of a dozen vessels, most of them wooden ships, and some of very great age. Along the centre of the isthmus, a full two hundred yards back from the beach on either side, gigantic seas had built a solid windrow of ships' timbers and other wreckage.

Scattered amongst the bones of men's handiwork were the bones of the greatest of all living creatures – skulls, ribs, baleen plates, vertebrae of blue and fin whales. The skull of one blue whale, half buried in the shifting sand, was so vast it towered over the tallest of us, and there was room on its broad crest for six people to sit in comfort and drink a respectful toast to a vanished giant.

It was with difficulty that Théo marshalled us back to *Oregon*. It was past time for us to go, because the tide had already begun to fall as we drove through the shoals to the mouth of the Barachois and into its narrow entrance.

The place was truly magical. There was a faint almost intangible mist although the sun burned clear above us. Distant objects wavered and grew unreal in a combination of mirage and haze. The mercury surface of the broad lagoon shimmered in strange patterns, the cause of which was not at once apparent to us. It was only when *Oregon* had fought her way, fishtailing like a salmon, through the entry against the swirling outflow that we could see and identify hundreds of sleek, black heads bobbing up and down, each sending out its own spreading cosmos of silvered ripples.

Miquelon's great lagoon belongs to seals – to the big, gentle grey seals. Their rookeries once gave life to a thousand off-shore islands and reefs from Labrador south to Cape Hatteras, but the grey seals fell easy prey to man, not because they are stupid but because they are possessed of remarkable innocence combined with great curiosity. For more than fifty years their only remaining haven was the Grand Barachois. Now, under protection, small colonies have moved out from this place to reoccupy some of their old haunts. Meanwhile the Barachois harbours as many as three thousand of them, young and old.

The Barachois is shoal, being nowhere more than three feet deep at low tide, and its bottom is the home of millions of clams that provide an inexhaustible food supply for the seals, and an infallible source of codfish bait for St. Pierre fishermen. Shell piles thirty feet tall, rising like white pyramids in the unclear distance, testified to the wealth of the lagoon.

At low tide two-thirds of the Barachois dries out in a random pattern of sand and mudbanks, with narrow and extremely shoal channels full of racing waters running between them. As we entered, the tops of the banks were just beginning to emerge, and Théo had to use all his skill and knowledge to find and to stay in the channels.

The rest of us were free to stare with incredulity at the myriad seals that rose around us and stared back. They were of all ages and all sizes, from pups of the year that thrust their wrinkled faces up to peer myopically at us from a few yards away, to ancient bulls weighing at least four hundred pounds that stood on their tail flippers, raising their bodies high out of the water to glare at us with a hint of challenge.

As the dory galumphed its way along, the seals gathered from distant parts of the lagoon until we were surrounded by them. The current-roiled waters were filled with twitching whiskers and pop-eyes. We passed one partly exposed bank upon which more than a hundred had already hauled out to sunbathe. They turned as one to watch us pass, but the day was too drowsy for action and they soon went back to sleep.

It took Théo an hour to wend his way to the northern

shore, under the loom of the Miquelon mountains, where Martin had a little hunting cabin. Here our passengers debarked, but we three crewmen had no time to go ashore. The tide was falling fast and we knew that if we did not immediately escape we would be marooned in the middle of the watery waste for ten hours or more. We fled for the entrance of the lagoon.

Because the St. Pierre and Miquelon dories must be beached each night their owners have invented a remarkable method of protecting the shafts and propellers. The shaft is equipped with a universal joint at the point where it descends through the bottom of the boat; and toward the stern there is a wooden-walled well. When a dory approaches shoal water, a handle protruding from this well is hauled upward and the propeller and shaft are lifted into the well, leaving the bottom clean of all protuberances.

As Théo sniffed for a passage where none seemed to exist, he delegated me to stand by the handle and, at his warning shout, to haul the propeller up before it struck bottom. Several times we lost the channels and drifted in three or four inches of water over the bars, but always we found another channel with sufficient depth to permit us to lower the propeller and put the engine back to work.

Then, halfway to the entry, I was just a trifle slow in answering Théo's bellow. There was a shuddering impact, the engine stopped, and we found ourself disabled.

We still had oars – or sweeps – massive fifteen-foot things, one of which was as much as a man could handle. However St. Pierre was twenty miles or more away. I assumed we would row back to Martin's shack from which point a ten-mile overland walk would have taken one of us to Miquelon, to arrange for a tow or perhaps to procure replacement parts.

I did not know Théophile Detcheverry. We rowed, if that is the word for manipulating the huge sweeps between their wooden thole-pins, the other way. We rowed and we rowed, frequently grounding, until we reached the entrance channel. Here we anchored in deep water in order to examine the damage.

Since *Oregon* was far too heavy to permit the three of us to haul her out and, since Théo could not swim, and I was too much of a gentleman to delegate the job to Claire, I stripped off my clothing and went diving. The water was bitterly cold but crystal clear. My first dive showed me that the propeller shaft was hopelessly bent. This, together with other damage, was beyond our means of repair. The best I could do was to attempt to release the shaft, so that the propeller could be hauled up into its housing out of the way.

This took some time and it attracted an audience. During my third dive I found myself staring, from a range of three feet, at a large, female, grey seal. At least I assumed it was a female, for it seemed to take an intense and uninhibited interest in me, thrusting its inquisitive head so close that, in my nudity, I would have blushed had I been able. Not being able (because I was blue with cold), I swam ashore where I stood, shivering and indignant, trying to explain my predicament to Claire and Théo. They were unsympathetic. Théo assured me that, in my semi-frozen state, I would be quite secure from sexual molestation. Claire merely smirked.

I went back to work and this time there were three seals waiting to give me a hand, or whatever it was they had in mind. Turning my back on them I finally freed the propeller, surfaced, and climbed aboard.

"You see," said Théo, and I think he was a little disappointed, "nothing happened, eh?"

I was at a loss to guess what Théo planned to do next but he soon told us. "Maintenant," he said firmly, "we sail home!"

I had not known we had a sail – and *what* a sail it proved to be. I think it must have belonged originally to a Greek trireme for it was of unbelievable antiquity. Of leg-of-mutton cut, it was so thin and sere that what wind there was (and there was hardly more than a zephyr) blew right through it.

With the aid of the sweeps we bucked out through the wild rip, where the incoming swell met the outgoing tide, until we were again in the open ocean.

Now the shore mist, which had seemed so lovely while

we were in the Barachois, became an enemy, for it obscured the low line of the dunes and dissolved the images of Mique-lon and Langlade. We were soon alone upon an empty ocean with no land in sight.

Not that there was any reason to worry about getting lost. *Oregon* did have a compass. Théo proudly produced it from under the thwart and casually set it on top of the engine hatch – on top of three hundred pounds of iron. The compass must have been, I think, Chinese, circa twelfth century. Its cover glass was so sand-etched that it was impossible to read the card. However since the pivot and the card were rusted into one, this hardly signified. The fact was we *had* a compass. Théo never looked at it, which may have been just as well.

Oregon sailed on. The sail kept falling down as its rotten halyards snapped. Then the lashings on the boom began to part. That sail was down for repairs more often than it was up. No matter. We idled in a generally southerly direction with a growing sense of unreality and, strangely, of content-ment. We should have been distraught but we were not. We stretched full length on the hatch boards in the late after-noon sun, drank wine, ate *pâté de foie gras*, chatted, snoozed, and whiled the time away with a lack of concern that, in retrospect, is difficult to explain. We might well have whiled away an entire infinity of time – had not the wind begun to shift. Mysteriously, it began to swing until it had gone through a full one hundred and eighty degrees, and had settled into the southeast.

Théo and I exchanged glances, although we said nothing aloud. There was no point in speaking our thoughts to Claire, but both of us knew that such a switch, at such a season of the year, under such conditions as had prevailed all day, meant storm.

I was not much worried even then. There was something about Théo's craggy certainty and something about the endur-ing qualities of *Oregon* that banished fear. Even if we were in for a blow I felt sure *Oregon* would weather it. Nevertheless, I was glad when the shore mist vanished and we found ourselves in sight of Langlade, and about five miles off its shores.

We could get no closer to the land because *Oregon*, having no keel, would not sail to weather. The wind was now rising briskly on our starboard beam and the sail, shrunken by repeated repairs into a mere rag, was moving us along at two or three knots. We were going generally in the direction of St. Pierre and were not dissatisfied with our progress, until Théo gestured with his head and I looked astern. The grey-black loom of fog was rolling in across the hills of Langlade, rolling implacably toward us.

At this juncture the rotten mast broke in half. We could have jury-rigged a sweep to take its place, but Théo vetoed this. The sweeps were needed. We would now, he told us, row to the eastward, until we gained shelter from the approaching storm under the lee of Langlade's cliffs.

So row we did, and made pathetically little progress for the current was setting off the land. And then we saw another motor dory hugging the shore under Anse aux Soldats, and going hell-bent for the beach at Grande Rivière. Claire promptly climbed up on our engine hatch and began waving Théo's yellow oilskin jacket on the end of a boathook. She waved it bravely, but either the distant dory did not see us, or was in too much of a hurry to reach shelter herself to come to our assistance.

The fog began pouring off the cliffs of Langlade and soon that island vanished. Théo and I rowed. God, how we rowed! The fog rolled closer, a scant two miles away, and we knew we were not going to make it to shore. Then Claire leapt to her feet again, balanced herself precariously, and began to wave her flag so furiously I thought she would go overboard. She had heard the distant mutter of another engine. We rested for a moment and listened too. Then, very faintly, we saw the shape of a vessel at the edge of the fog bank. She was making knots toward St. Pierre.

Now we all waved, and Théo roared. I blew a huge conch

horn that was normally used for a fog warning. The stranger vessel held to her course, entered the fog bank, disappeared, and then miraculously reappeared heading directly for us.

She was the *St. Eugène*, a big power launch belonging to the commune of St. Pierre and used as a passenger boat between that place and Miquelon. When she came alongside and took our tow-rope, her skipper told us that neither he nor any member of his crew had seen or heard us. However an old woman (the widow of a dory fisherman lost on the Plate Banks many years earlier), who was sitting wrapped in a blanket in the stern, thought she glimpsed a boat far out to sea. She was ignored until she became so insistent that, despite his own anxiety to reach port, the skipper turned back out of the fog to set her mind at rest.

He also told us that the first hurricane warning of the season had been issued, and all shipping had been advised to seek shelter immediately.

To say that Claire and I were happy to be under tow would be an understatement; but Théo was not at all happy. While I took the tiller he stood amidship, arms crossed, head hunched forward between his massive shoulders, ignoring the good-natured banter from the crew of the *St. Eugène*, and seemingly unaware of the world around him. For him this was ignominy. For the first time in his seafaring life he had been forced to take a tow.

Sea and wind were rising fast as we rounded Colombier. We never saw its towering cliffs because by then the fog had become an all-embracing shroud. As we entered the channel, *St. Eugène* slowed till she barely had steerage way, and we became aware that the black fog on every side was alive with ships. Their sirens and fog-horns sounded all around us, and they began looming up ahead, astern, abeam, until we seemed to be completely hemmed in. They were Spanish trawlers, sixty of them, feeling their way in by radar from the Grand Banks on the wings of the hurricane warning.

Théo and two of his sons hauled *Oregon* high on her slip. Claire and I went off to drink and eat, and to be happy we were ashore upon a solid rock, as the hurricane began to whine and whistle through the chimney-tops of St. Pierre.

Théophile did not join us. He spent that entire night out in the open, in the wind, in driving walls of rain, repairing his beloved dory. That was the kind of man he was: Churchill and Rommel both.

16· *The game is played*

ONE OF THE THINGS the Manuel brothers impressed upon me during our meeting in Miquelon was that St. Pierre harboured R.C.M.P. informers. These spies reported the departure of all suspicious vessels by shortwave radio to police cutters lurking outside French territorial waters. Because of this, most Newfoundland boats engaging in the game chose to make their runs to and from Miquelon but, for reasons which will appear, it was necessary for *Itchy* to make her departure from St. Pierre.

It was not easy to keep our intentions secret. Not only did most St. Pierrais seem to be privy to our plans from the outset, but a number of them tried to become personally involved.

One day at the dark of noon Jean, Martin, Frederico, François, and several other acquaintances made their surreptitious way across the Place, pausing to let a squad of gendarmes (who were practising a march-past) go by, before sneaking aboard our boat, unobserved except by about a third of the population of the town.

Each of them was carrying something. Frederico had a case of Lemon Hart 151 overproof rum, thinly disguised in newspapers. Martin had two demijohns of red wine wrapped in an old petticoat. Over his shoulder Jean carried a cotton sack through which the shapes of a dozen brandy bottles were plainly visible.

Mike, meeting them on deck, nearly had a fit. The mainsail had been hoisted in order to dry it out, and he had the presence of mind to let fly the halyards, bringing gaff and sail crashing down to conceal our visitors and their parcels under one lumpy, writhing mass of canvas.

These parcels were not an integral part of *our* cargo. They were gifts, which the donors hoped we would be obliging enough to deliver to friends of theirs in various Newfoundland outports.

Some necessary modifications to our vessel were carried out at an abandoned wharf on the far side of the harbour. With the help of Paulo and Théo, we built wooden troughs, twenty inches wide and twenty inches high, along each side of the cabin trunk. Each trough was fitted with cross-cleats, to hold our cargo in place, if we ran into rough weather. Strips of canvas lashed over the troughs were designed to protect the cargo from spray and rain.

The reason for storing the cargo on deck was, of course, so that it could be readily jettisoned if we were challenged by a police cutter. Here Paulo's genius came into play. He constructed a hinged system which would enable us, by means of a wooden lever, to tip each trough over its respective rail, so that we could rid ourselves of the whole of our cargo in a matter of seconds.

We were to take our departure from St. Pierre at 0400 hours, two hours before dawn, on the given day. Our course was to be almost due north until we were abeam of Miquelon, after which we would be in international waters where we could idle along secure from molestation until evening. At dusk, we were to move to the edge of Canadian territorial waters, three miles off Pass Island, which guards the eastern entrance to Hermitage Bay. Three or four skiffs from Selbys Cove would be waiting for us at this rendezvous, having spent the balance of the day jigging cod in the vicinity. In case we encountered fog, we were to locate the rendezvous by listening for the sound of a ten-gauge shotgun being fired at irregular intervals.

At dawn, on the day before our departure, Théo went off to sea for a day's fishing. He caught no fish. Instead he visited a friend at Soldier Bay, from whom he acquired fourteen bags of "insurance" for our cargo. Théo had previously cached the cargo itself – fourteen crates of it – in a cave near Cap Percé. Just after dark he stopped at this cave and recovered the cases, before proceeding with great caution back to St. Pierre. He had need of caution. *Oregon* was so grossly overloaded that if Théo had leaned over the side to spit he would probably have capsized her then and there.

It was, naturally, a foggy night. The certainty of fog was one of the few things we were able to rely upon. It was also raining a little, and conditions were sufficiently miserable that even the intrepid St. Pierrais preferred to stay at home, or in the warmth of the bars. The last visitor left the dock where we were lying shortly before midnight.

At 0300 hours Mike and Paulo and I were sitting in the cabin, nervously nipping, when there came a gentle bump alongside. We hustled on deck to meet a grinning and per-spiring Théo. He had stopped his engine opposite the Hard (as any returning fisherman would normally have done), and then had rowed the heavily laden boat into the inner harbour to our berth.

There was more rowing still to do; but first we trans-shipped the cargo, stowing it in the troughs and battening it down under the canvas covers. Then we silently cast off our moorings and gave *Oregon* a tow rope. Mike and Paulo joined Théo in the dory to help him man the sweeps, leaving me to steer *Itchy*.

I will never know how Théo found his way across the harbour, out the entrance, and down the North Channel; but after an hour the tow-line slackened and *Itchy* drifted along-side *Oregon*. In a hoarse whisper Théo told us we were at the mouth of the North Channel and had nothing ahead of us but open sea. It was then 0400 hours and time for us to part, but somehow I did not feel like parting. I made the excuse that we had all better have a farewell drink. We would maybe have had a second, had we not been transfixed by a booming voice coming out of the fog from a few feet away.

"How long you fellows going to fool around? You want to wait until the sun comes up?"

The voice belonged to our old friend, the Chief Pilot of St. Pierre. He had with him three or four cronies. They had come out to make sure that Théo's navigation was up to snuff and to be on hand to wish us luck.

Mike hoisted the sails. A southerly zephyr filled the unseen canvas and the vessel began to move. *Oregon* let slip our line and vanished. We were alone – almost. Out of the Stygian darkness came a final admonition from the Pilot.

"Don't forget, steer half a point to nor'ard of your course when you get clear of the Plate Rock. Big tide running out of Hermitage Bay will set you off to eastward." So much for secrecy in St. Pierre.

We sailed for an hour in order to be reasonably sure we were out of earshot of the islands before starting the bullgine. Jean-Pierre had done a good job on her but he had failed to muffle her thunderous voice.

The voyage north past Miquelon was uneventful; in truth, it was tedious. We steered a compass course. Periodically we stopped the bullgine and hauled the patent log to check the distance run, after which we listened hard for several minutes. We heard nothing except once the mew of an unseen gull. Dawn came and the fog lightened, becoming opalescent grey instead of charcoal black. Our world was again a fog-bounded hemisphere, a hundred feet in radius, in which we did not really seem to move at all. Yet by ten o'clock we had logged thirty nautical miles, and were only twenty from our rendezvous.

We were by then in international waters where we had no reason to be apprehensive about a confrontation with the R.C.M.P. Being sticklers for the letter of the law themselves, they were not likely to attempt an act of piracy by boarding us "on the high seas." However we were well aware they had radar – excellent military radar – with which they could detect and follow us miles away, while we could not hope to detect them until they were alongside us.

We decided to stop the engine and lie-to until it was time to steam toward the rendezvous. But here a problem arose; one that I had not previously considered. Our navigation was entirely by dead reckoning; by compass course and distance logged. We had no other way of knowing where we were. Once stopped, we would begin to drift with the currents that run along Newfoundland's south coast, and we would have no way of telling how far, or in what direction we were drifting. When we again started the motor and got under way we would be proceeding from an unknown point, with no true idea of the distance or direction to our destination.

When I confided this difficulty to Mike he reacted in a manner that suggested he was not yet quite ready to take his papers as a master mariner.

"If it's only the drift you're worried about, Farley, why don't we just throw a chip of wood overboard and see which way *it* moves. Then we'll know which way *we're* drifting."

That was one of the longest days I ever spent at sea. We sat there, somewhere in the Atlantic, from ten o'clock until nearly five o'clock. For a wonder the sea remained calm.

There was not even a swell to give the illusion of life in a dead world. We saw and heard no living thing. The silence became so oppressive that we brought the little transistor radio on deck, and listened with actual gratitude to whining imitation cowboy songs. Still, the time barely dripped away. Seconds became minutes and minutes hours. I felt a tearing impatience to get the engine started and to head for where I hoped Pass Island might still be found.

At a quarter to five I could stand it no longer. "Start her up," I told Mike. "We'll go in slow. If we get there too early we can always stop and wait again."

It was a fantastic relief to be under way, even though I was now by no means sure of the correct course to steer. We stopped the engine every half hour and stood on listening watch, in the hopes of hearing the powerful fog-horn on Pass Island. It did not prove powerful enough. We never heard it.

At 6:52 we stopped the engine for the fourth time. And at 6:52:01 we heard the hard rumble of big diesel engines close on our starboard bow!

Although we had schooled ourselves to endure just such a shock as this, our psychological preparations proved to be inadequate. The sound only lasted a few seconds and then was abruptly silenced, but neither of us was able to move a muscle for what seemed like an eternity. How long we held our immobility I cannot say, but just as we were both beginning to think we had been the victims of a trick of acoustics a God-almighty siren went off right in my ear.

It was the loudest and most hideous noise I have ever heard. It was a blaring agony of sound that all the cab drivers in New York, gathered together and sounding their horns in one manic rage, could never equal. It was appalling! It was also unmistakable – there was no room for doubt about its ownership.

Mike and I responded with a pure Pavlovian reflex. I flew to the port trough and Mike to the starboard one. We stripped the lashings off like so much tissue paper, flipped the locking lugs, and hauled back on the levers. Bags and crates went overboard with a single colossal splash. We collided in the companionway as we both dived below to jettison through the portholes six bottles of more-or-less legitimate rum, plus two corkscrews and a bottle opener!

Our duty done, we sat and waited. For a good ten minutes there was not a sound of any kind, then there was the rumble of diesels starting up. The sound crept closer and died to a slow mutter.

"Hey," asked a husky voice, "anybody on that boat?"

Lying alongside, with her big bows towering high above us, was the R.C.M.P. *Blue Iris*. Grouped around her machine-gun were half a dozen policemen, made up to look like sailors. They were smiling.

Their leader, captain, inspector, or whatever the R.C.M.P. call their skippers, was smiling widest of all.

"Thought you was the *Marie Céleste*," he said cheerfully. "Don't you fellows know about fog-horns? You could have run us down if we hadn't been watching you on radar for the last few hours. Where ya going anyway?"

I have previously noted that Mike was possessed of an extraordinarily quick mind. He broke into fluent Spanish, waved his hands and arms wildly, rolled his eyes, and pointed to the outlandish name written large upon our bows, and to the garish Basque flag that hung despondently from the main truck.

Taking the cue, I added my bit.

"Es Baska sheep amigos, hasta la vista, adios, oui, oui, si, si, si!"

For a moment the policemen looked thoroughly bewildered then, concluding with true Anglo-Saxon arrogance that we could not understand *their* language, they broke into talk amongst themselves.

"Holy Jehoshaphat, will you listen to them Frogs!" one of them said.

"Sure scared the ass clean off them, anyway," another added.

"Yeah. Made them dump their load so quick I bet they never had time to think. What a sick bunch they're going to be when they find out they was six miles off Pass Island and three outside the legal limit!"

Up to this point I had not harboured any personal ill will toward these men. But at this revelation I got mad. Abandoning my Spanish role, I unleashed all the vitriol at my command:

"Why, you red-coated tomato-livered pisspots!" I began. "You . . . ." But there may be youngsters listening.

The policemen blanched visibly. Then the leader found his voice.

"You cut that out!" he yelled. "You just watch your lip, buddy! We're on to your salt-bag tricks. If you think your chums hanging about in them boats over there," and here he pointed fiercely off to starboard, "are going to get a drop of that stuff you dumped, you better think again. We're staying right here until it all comes up and we'll sink every bloody case. All right, Jones! Back her off. Let's get clear of this stinkbox!"

The *Blue Iris*'s mighty engines thundered and she went astern, vanishing almost instantly into the foggy murk.

As soon as she was out of sight Mike turned to me and I to him – and we grinned at each other like a pair of idiots.

No, we had not gone out of our minds. The truth was we had a lot to grin about. In the first place we now knew approximately where we were, and where the Manuels were awaiting us. And in the second place, but, wait a minute . . . .

We started the bullgine and steered cautiously to the eastward for an hour. When we again stopped and listened we had not long to wait before hearing the dull boom of a heavy shot-gun. Fifteen minutes later we saw the shadow of a boat. It was the Manuel brothers' big trap skiff. It, and three more like it, were anchored on the Pass Island Banks. All four skiffs hauled their grapnels and clustered close about us.

Almon was the first aboard, and as I shook his big, hard paw, his bright blue gaze took in our empty decks. He did not need to be told what had happened.

"Hard luck, skipper!" he said, and chuckled.

"They caught us fair and square, the bastards," I replied

bravely. "About six miles to the sou'west of here. We had to dump the works. And they intend to stay right there until the stuff comes up."

By this time half a dozen other burly fishermen had swarmed aboard. They heard my sorrowful tale and they could not contain their feelings. They began to giggle, to guffaw, to whack each other on the back with man-killing blows.

"It's not *that* bloody funny," I said, when I could get a word in edgewise. "We overdid things a bit and dumped our own stock over too."

"Me son, me darlin' man," said Hondas when he could speak through the tears of laughter streaming down his cheeks, "dat's what *I* calls makin' a good try onto it! But don't you worry none. You lads'll not go dry this night!"

Nor did we. Abandoning our sunken cargo to the tenacious lads on the *Blue Iris* we got under way. Piloted by Almon, we motored down into Hermitage Bay. Three hours later *Itchy* lay snugly at anchor in Selbys Cove and Mike and I were enjoying the hospitality of the little village. It proved to be as "wet" as Hondas had prophesied it would be. We went from house to house, and at each we had to tell our tale again, and at each we were solaced with alky and hot water.

About two o'clock in the morning, by which time the party had engulfed the entire village, a young man came running into Hondas Manuel's house, his face alight with excitement.

"They're a-coming in!" he cried. "I hears them, byes!"

En masse, the villagers made for the community stage at the foot of the little cove. Mike and I were swept along with them. The muted mutter of engines was strong in the dark night. A light glimmered briefly in the fog and then, one by one, the three big trap skiffs we had met earlier on the Pass Island Banks appeared out of the black mist and ran alongside the stage.

They were log-loaded. Between them they must have held at least forty cases plus a dozen kegs.

The cargo that was lovingly unloaded from the skiffs was

the real stuff; whereas the cargo *we* had carried from St. Pierre consisted of fourteen wooden cases – filled with rocks – ballasted with fourteen salt bags – filled with sand. Our role, as determined for us by the Hondas brothers, had been that of a stalking horse charged with deflecting and preoccupying the hounds of the law, and so leaving the skiffs that had waited for us off Pass Island free to make their unobstructed ways to Miquelon and back again, untroubled by interference from *Blue Iris*.

As Hondas remarked to us, after thanking us on behalf of all the thirsty folk of Hermitage Bay:

"They's more an one way to skin a cod . . . or cod a Mountie; and we'se the byes what knows 'em all!"

17 · *Westward No!*

We DID NOT linger in Selbys Cove – departing well before noon – and giving Pass Island Banks a wide berth. We saw nothing of *Blue Iris*. Presumably she was still hovering over the sunken kegs, like a broody hen guarding a batch of infertile eggs.

Itchy's performance on this voyage had been exemplary. She had done everything we asked of her and had produced no unsettling surprises. Of course she still leaked, but we had grown accustomed to this, and the hourly pumping routine had become so automatic we could almost do it in our sleep. At long last she seemed ready to set out on a major voyage, but it was too late. Mike had outrun his time and, having established as many branch libraries on the Newfoundland coast as the circumstances allowed, had reluctantly to take his departure and return to St. John's.

I spent another week in St. Pierre, toying with the idea of shipping Paul or Théo as mate for a voyage to the Caribbean, but the hurricane season had begun, and when the next bad blow sank two large fishing vessels on the St. Pierre Bank, I was persuaded that the Grand Voyage should be deferred until another year.

Having resolved to leave *Itchy* in St. Pierre for the winter, I enlisted Théo, Paulo, and Martin to look after her, suppos-

ing that three godfathers would be three times as good as one. I instructed them to have her hauled on the slip and safely stored ashore until it was time to launch her in the spring. Then I returned to the mainland and to a winter of routine, buoyed up by dreams of the coming summer.

This time Jack McClelland could not share my dreams. Rumours about *Itchy*'s antics had reached the ears of his business associates and members of his family, none of whom considered him expendable.

"If I could afford to quadruple my insurance coverage," Jack explained sadly, "I imagine there'd be very little objection to my sailing with you. But there's no way I can afford the premiums my agent wants. He says they'd be cheaper if I were going to make a lunar voyage in a Yankee rocket."

I was not too disappointed. Much as I admired Jack, I had developed an ever greater admiration for the young lady who had been, for a brief period, a member of my crew at St. Pierre. My discovery that Claire would be available, aye, and ready, to make a cruise with me during the coming summer did much to alleviate my distress at Jack's defection.

I had no word about *Itchy* during the winter but this did not disturb me because none of my St. Pierre friends was much at letter writing. However in May I received a vaguely worded cablegram from Martin. The gist of it was that there had been a small accident and *Itchy* had "pierced herself," but was "not much hurted" and, I gathered, could easily be repaired. I guessed there had been a minor mishap during the launching. Feeling full confidence in my three friends I cabled a reply ordering repairs to be made forthwith and, oh depths of foolishness, informing Martin that the schooner was well-insured.

In mid-June I headed east. A groaning old Dakota aircraft deposited me, with a belly-shaking jolt, on the cow pasture at St. Pierre.

To my surprise (for I had cabled advance notice of my coming) none of my friends was on hand to greet me. When I set out to find them it was like trying to locate a grain of uranium without a Geiger counter. Everyone I talked to seemed singularly evasive; even somewhat anxious to get away from my company. Much puzzled, I sought out the incomparable Ella Girardin at L'Escal and from her received the first hints that all was not well with my little ship. She told me enough to send me streaking for the shipyard.

My poor little vessel was still high on the slip. She looked like an antediluvian monster that had just been fished out of the La Brea tar pits. She was enslimed from the tops of her masts to the bottom of her keel with foul black muck that stank like a sewage farm. Her decks seemed inches thick in the stuff and her cabin was more like the inside of a septic tank than a home for people. Most shocking of all was the condition of her stern. A good six feet of it seemed to have been chewed off, leaving her looking as pathetic as a duck that has backed into a high-speed fan.

I was standing, dazed, below her ruptured stern when one of the dockyard workers passed by. He did not stop, but after nodding his head at the mutilated and encrusted vessel he took his nose meaningfully between thumb and forefinger. At that gesture I saw red. I went looking for Paul, *or* Théo, *or* Martin, with the purposefulness of a Malay villager running amok.

I did not find Théo – he was believed to be in Miquelon. I did not find Martin – he was supposed to be camping somewhere on Langlade. I did not find Paulo – he was reputed to have shipped aboard a freighter for the West Indies. However, after three days of fury and frustration, I *did* find enough wisps and fragments of the story to be able to piece them together into a coherent whole.

What had happened was, in a sense, my own fault. In asking three men to take charge of *Itchy* I had revealed a monumental ignorance of the Gallic temperament. Each felt that he alone should have been put in full command and the result was that none of the three did anything. The schooner was left to spend the winter at anchor in the harbour, unloved and unregarded, while my three friends waged war amongst themselves. Nobody *won* that war – but *Itchy* and I assuredly lost it.

Somehow she survived the fall and winter gales. Then, in early March, the arctic pack-ice beset the islands. A few days later a westerly gale drove the ice solidly into the harbour. The pressure broke the hold of *Itchy*'s anchors and she was driven, stern first, against the projecting timbers of an abandoned wharf. One of the timbers pierced her counter and she went down in three fathoms of filth; for the inner harbour at St. Pierre is nothing more nor less than a sewage basin for the whole community.

Martin, Théo, and Paulo were distraught but spent their energies in useless recriminations against each other. *Itchy* stayed on the bottom, sinking deeper and deeper into the slime, until the receipt in St. Pierre of my cable containing the magic word "insured."

St. John's, Newfoundland, does not hold a monopoly on mercantile piracy. St. Pierre, much as I love the place, has its own breed of brigands, and when word got around that *Itchy* was insured, they went into action. A group of them refloated the vessel (using oil drums that were lashed alongside her and then pumped full of air) and took possession of her as a right of salvage. They had her hauled on the slip, nominally for repairs, but when they discovered she only needed cleaning out and the replacement of one plank in her counter, they arranged to increase the repair costs by the simple expedient of tearing off six feet of her stern with crowbars.

The "repairs" were not undertaken immediately, as I had ordered, because the shipyard had enough work to do and it was felt it would be more thrifty to save *Itchy* for a slack period. She was still being saved when I arrived.

I am not particularly proud of my behaviour during the several weeks that followed, but then I am not particularly proud of the way the St. Pierrais behaved either. We fought. We fought bitterly, continuously, cunningly, and sometimes viciously. It took six weeks for me to get the boat ready for sea again. It was a black period of obstruction, misery, and near madness as I wrestled with brigandage and venality; harbour muck and shipyard sloth.

I can only recall two bright moments. One was when, in a state of blind fury, I forced my way into the office of the governor of the islands and had the pleasure of calling His Excellency an s.o.b. (he refrained from having me arrested, as he might reasonably have done, contenting himself with having me frog-marched out the door). The other bright moment was when the pirates presented me with their bills for salvage and repairs and I not only refused to sign them on behalf of the insurance company, but publicly recommended (with appropriate gestures) that they use the bills to relieve a temporary shortage of absorbent paper which was then plaguing the islands.

This dark interlude came to an end in the last week of July when Claire arrived. Suddenly the sun shone (quite literally: there had been almost constant fog since my arrival). *Itchy* was moderately clean again (although we kept finding deposits of St. Pierre sewage in hidden corners for the next several months); she had been fitted with a new and reliable diesel engine, replacing the horrible bullgine; her bunks had been enlarged, and she was at least as tight as she had ever been. Claire's presence dissolved the bitterness in my soul and I sought out my erstwhile St. Pierre friends and made my peace with them.

Martin, Théo, and Paul (who had not really gone to the West Indies) were so relieved at the rapprochement that they threw a party for us. It was a good party, and when Claire and I set out to return to *Itchy* – launched now, and lying alongside Paulo's boat again – we were in a gay mood.

I have not previously mentioned that *Itchy* lacked toilet facilities. The truth is that I had never thought about installing them because, until Claire's coming, they would have been redundant. The bob chains forward, and the bumpkin aft, provided adequate comfort in an open-air environment. For men.

Having boarded the ship I went below to light the lamps, leaving Claire the privacy of the dark and slippery decks. Soon I heard a mammoth splash and rushed on deck with a flashlight to find her small, white face bobbing in the black, oily waters alongside. She was not alone. A few feet away my flashlight beam picked up the grinning gape of a cat that had died hard, and died a long, long time ago. Fortunately Claire had sense enough to keep her mouth shut. Had she swallowed any of the water of the inner harbour it is possible my story would have ended on a tragic note.

Rescuing her was something of a task because, as she pointed out when she was finally dragged, dripping and furious, on to the deck, "Nobody can swim with their slacks down around their ankles!" In truth, she must have found it a harrowing experience, but when she had been taken up to Paulo's, hot-bathed, fortified with brandy, and given clean clothes, her good nature reasserted itself. In fact, I was so pleased with her that I redesigned the forepeak of the schooner so that there would be room for a small convenience, "Ladies, for the use of."

Although the general situation in St. Pierre had now become comparatively pleasant, there was one sore spot left and it grew steadily worse until it threatened to erupt into serious trouble. The local pirates were demanding immediate payment in full, and were adamantly opposed to a negotiated settlement. I, on the other hand, was equally determined not to authorize payment of a single sou until they modified their demands. Things came to a head when an *avocat* appeared on board to tell me that unless I paid up, and at once, he would slap a blanket on the schooner. This is a nautical phrase, which means the arrest of a boat and her delivery into the hands of a bailiff.

My reaction can be imagined. I had already lost almost two months' sailing time because of the machinations of the St. Pierrais, and I was double-damned if I was going to lose so much as another day. Nor was I going to pay what amounted to an exorbitant ransom for *Itchy's* freedom. I devised a counter-ploy.

Under the pretext of testing the new engine I announced my intention of making a short run down the North Channel.

To allay suspicions (the pirates were a deeply suspicious lot who kept *Itchy* under close scrutiny), I did not apply at the customs-house for a clearance. I *did* invite several island friends to come along for a joy ride; their presence being calculated to guarantee that I was not about to make a break for far horizons.

Only one St. Pierrais was privy to my real intentions – not that I couldn't trust the discretion of my other friends (I couldn't), but because I did not need their witting help. The man whose co-operation I required (and to protect the guilty he shall remain nameless), was under sufficient obligation to me to warrant my trust.

Early in the morning we let go our lines and motored gaily out of the harbour. Half an hour later, off Colombier, we encountered a dory that was apparently experiencing engine trouble. I put *Itchy* alongside, and informed my surprised guests that they had better board the dory immediately – unless they wanted to be carried to Nova Scotia, whither, I told them, I was now bound. They were so dumbfounded they departed with only token protests.

Itchy had only three miles to go to escape from French territorial waters, and within the hour we were safe on the high seas. My one regret is that I was not present when the brigand band discovered we had escaped them.

The bills were eventually settled – after two years of argument. The sum paid by the insurance company was about a third what had been demanded. It may be thought I would never dare show my face on St. Pierre again. Not so. When I returned three years after the event to make a film about the islands, one of the worst of the pirates was the first man to buy me a drink. Far from holding a grudge, these gentlemen welcomed me like a returning prodigal. Being a WASP, born and bred, I suppose I will *never* understand the Gallic point of view.

As a result of the spring mix-up, plans for the season's voyage had to be radically altered. There was not sufficient time remaining to allow for a major off-shore voyage. Also there was the fact that Claire, smart and able as she was, could only be classed as a "green hand," not yet ripe enough to dare the ocean main. I therefore proposed that we spend what was left of the summer cruising west along the southern coast of Newfoundland with Cape Breton, Nova Scotia, as our objective. Cape Breton, being Scots, seemed like a safe place to leave *Itchy* for the winter, as well as representing an ideal departure point for a major voyage the following year.

Beyond the stark reefs called Les Enfants Perdus we hoisted sail and made a pleasant passage across Fortune Bay, skirting Pass Island, and holding to the west until we were well clear of the area usually patrolled by *Blue Iris*. Policemen have long memories, and their sense of humour cannot always be relied upon.

Probably because I had forgotten to pour the customary libation to the Old Man, the weather turned against us, and a sou'west storm forced us to run for the shelter of Pushthrough, a little outport lying at the western mouth of a maze of great fiords called Bay d'Espoir.

This diversion proved to be a fatal move as far as our plans were concerned. Blinding fog and/or sou'west gales and pouring rain kept us glued to the Pushthrough wharf. There we entertained many local residents, one of whom told us how the place got its name.

The settlement is divided into two parts by a narrow channel, or tickle. One night, long, long ago, a giant blue whale made the mistake of trying to take a shortcut through the tickle, and got stranded. *He* was in trouble, but so were the human residents. They knew that if he died and decomposed where he was, there would be no living in the place for years to come. Either he or the people had to go. After some futile attempts to tow him out backwards with rowboats (there were no engines in those days) the entire population waded out into the tickle – and pushed him through.

Pushthrough gave Claire her first experience of housekeeping on a small boat under conditions of real adversity. Because *Itchy*'s decks were almost as porous as her hull, the interior of the cabin quickly became saturated, and stayed that way through the next seven days of almost constant rain and fog. An astounding variety of moulds and other fungi began to flourish in the cabin. Claire's *sotto voce* comments as she scraped an inch of green fuzz off the bacon, the bread, or the butter, suggested that her private school education had been much more catholic in content than I had previously suspected.

On the day she found a thick layer of gelatinous blue mould inside her slippers *after* she had put them on her bare feet, she surpassed herself. I lay on my soggy bunk and chortled, until she rounded on me.

"Go ahead," she snarled. "Laugh your fool head off! And when you get done, take a look at yourself in the mirror."

Intrigued, I wiped the moisture off the mirror and peered into it. There was no doubt about it: my reddish beard had developed a distinctly greenish cast.

For fear of becoming fungi-food before our time, we fled from Pushthrough into the fog-and-storm-free inner fiords of Bay d'Espoir, seeking warmth and sunshine. We found both, and as we penetrated deeper into the mysterious recesses of the bay we became so enamoured of its many inlets, hidden harbours, rock-walled runs, and majestic scenery that it was not until the end of August that we bethought ourselves of continuing our western voyage.

The bay is called Bay d'Espoir only on modern maps; to the people who live near it, it is Bay Despair. But its original name was Bay d'Esprit, given to it perhaps four hundred years ago by French fishermen-settlers. This is a true name, for it is a haunted place—haunted by memories of the past when each of its innumerable coves held a handful of families of French, Jersey, English, or Micmac Indian origin; and haunted too by the pathetic shades of the Red Indians, the Beothuks, who were slaughtered to the last man, woman, and child by English settlers.

At the time we cruised its dark waters the great bay was almost devoid of human life. Pass-My-Can Island, Harbour le Gallais, Great Jervais, Roti Bay, Barasway de Cerf, The Locker, Snooks Cove, Jack Damp Cove, Lampidoes Passage—all, all were empty; an omen of the politically ordained future which will soon see most of Newfoundland's remaining people concentrated in a few score "industrial," and mostly inland, towns on the modern urban model.

Only at Head of the Bay, forty miles from the open sea that once gave them their life and sustenance, were there any people. And this was truly Bay Despair. Here in the depressed villages of Milltown, St. Alban's, Morristown, were the descendants of the sea-dwellers, lured to these sad places decades ago by the labour recruiters of an international pulp and paper company which needed cheap labour in the woods. When the cream of the pulpwood had been cut, the company pulled out without a thought for the dislocated lives it was leaving behind. It is an old story, told too many times—still being told. The story of the manipulation of simple people, and the rape of the land itself, by men devoid of conscience.

Late in September, when we finally roused ourselves to make another attempt to sail westward toward Cape Breton, *Itchy* absolutely refused to co-operate.

Ever since she had rounded Cape Race on her maiden

voyage she had shown a singular reluctance to sail west. I think she may have guessed, from the first days when I became her owner, that it was my eventual intention to separate her from her native shores, and she had made up her mind to thwart me. It must have been so, for nothing else can possibly explain her behaviour whenever we turned her bows westward; or even *threatened* to do so.

On the day we planned to leave Head of the Bay *Itchy* refused to go into gear (the new engine was equipped with a three-speed gearbox). We took the whole gearbox apart – a mammoth task – and found not a thing at fault. When we reassembled it the gear shift worked, but *Itchy* had meanwhile slackened her keel fastenings and had begun to leak so prodigiously that we had no choice except to haul her out on the beach at Milltown.

And there we had to leave her for the winter.

The following summer we made another attempt to force her to the westward. Although she resisted mightily, we managed, by stubborn perseverance, to get her as far west as the island archipelago of Burgeo, about midway along the southwest coast, and some eighty miles from Bay d'Espoir. This struggle exhausted me in body and in spirit, and when, just off the Burgeo Islands, she literally pulled out all the stops and began to sink again, I headed in for the land in a state of sullen rage.

There were no facilities for hauling her out at Burgeo so we spent days frigging around trying to staunch the leaks from within, and making no progress. One morning we awoke to the realization that again the sailing season was at an end, and that we were not going to get *Itchy* an inch beyond Burgeo that year.

I have occasionally been accused of being pig-headed, but the epithet is undeserved. If I am anything, I am a moderate, calm, and reasonable man. Which is why I said to Claire:

"No bloody boat is going to beat *me*. If *she* stays here this winter, *we* stay too. We'll watch her like a hawk. And when spring comes I'll have her in such shape she won't be

able to pull any more of her damn tricks, at least until we get her to Nova Scotia. What do you say?"

"Why not?" said Claire, being the kind of woman who is game for anything.

I set about making arrangements for winter storage for the vessel, while Claire went off and found a house for us at Messers Cove, which lies on the western extremity of the Burgeo community.

The house she found was small and snug, perched on a bold rock overlooking the open sea where it was swept by living spray during sou'west gales. Claire also found a new member for our family. This was Albert, a young black water-dog from Grand Bruit; of the same lineage as Blanche, the shipyard dog of St. Pierre.

Some of the effects of our decision were remarkable. *Itchy* promptly stopped leaking (well, almost). For want of a place to haul her out, we had to moor her for the winter in a cove where there was a lot of ice movement; yet she went through the winter without taking the least damage and emerged in spring in perfect working order. From being our intractable and bloody-minded adversary, she had become a docile and loving little boat – until the June day we tried to start west again.

Despite my generous libations to the Old Man of the Sea, *Happy Adventure* (she had reverted to her original name) evidently had much more influence with him than I did. She used her influence shamelessly. Every time we put out from Burgeo we ran into westerly gales, impenetrable fog, massive seas, or all three at the same time. Furthermore, every time we tried to head west something went wrong with the engine, the rigging, the hull; or else the leaks reappeared as ship-born gushers.

After three weeks of constant defeats Claire and I felt we needed a rest and we decided to sail to the nearby settlement of Jerts Cove, huddled under the massive cliffs of the Grey River fiord. We intended to spend a few days visiting a friend who lived there, resting our bodies and restoring our spirits before again tackling the western voyage.

Grey River lies *east* of Burgeo and *Happy Adventure* went eastward as happily as a bird on the wing. But when we tried to return to Burgeo we ran into a heavy gale. *Happy Adventure* parted her forestay, dirt got into the injectors and killed the engine, and we were forced to turn and run before the wind and seas. We did not regain the land until we reached Richards Harbour, *sixty miles east of Burgeo.*

It was then the middle of July and I was beginning to realize how completely outclassed I was in this battle of wills. When we put out of Richards Harbour, and promptly lost our way (the compass began acting wildly) in a heavy fog, I resignedly let my stubborn little vessel have her head, and she took us into Bay d'Espoir. We bowed to fate and gave up the unequal battle for the year.

There are much worse fates than having to spend a summer in that seductive bay. As we became increasingly familiar with its intricacies we reaped special rewards. One of these was when we penetrated into Conne River, and encountered the last remaining settlement of Micmac Indians to live in Newfoundland. One couple, Michael John and his blind wife, adopted us, treating us as their own children. Michael, then nearing eighty, but still as tough as basalt, told us ageless tales of his people and of the vanished Red Indians—tales no white man had heard before, perhaps. He gave us a vivid but heart-breaking glimpse into an older world and, it may be, a better one than ours.

We also met again a certain robust pair of brothers from Hermitage Bay who were the only men actively fishing in Bay d'Espoir. Whenever we ran across them, which was often, they came alongside and loaded us up with redfish, lobsters, salmon, cod, and big sea trout. They also solved the problem arising from the absence of a convenient liquor store.

Bay d'Espoir fed us surpassingly well. In Harbour le Gallais we would strip off at low tide and wade about collecting blue mussels, horse mussels, soft-shelled clams, and dainty scallops, or we would borrow a few lobster pots and use them to catch a meal of crabs.

There was one particularly memorable occasion when we were moored in a glorious little harbour at Raymond Point. Late at night Claire and I were lying cosily on our bunks reading by lamplight. Albert had gone ashore and was sniffing and snoofing at the water's edge. We heard a mighty splash and a few moments later his claws clattered on the deck. He dropped something squishy in the cockpit, then went ashore, and again we heard a splash.

Curious, I climbed the companion ladder with a flashlight and was in time to meet him coming back aboard with a two-foot-long squid squirming in his mouth, its tentacles flailing in futile protest and curling limply around his ink-bespattered muzzle.

Great schools of squid were then running up the bay and Albert, being a fishing dog without prejudices, had decided to catch a mess of them. His procedure was to sit on the end of a nearby abandoned wharf and wait for the phosphorescent flash as a squid surfaced close to him. Then he leapt, a full-bodied dive that carried him far under the surface. He did not get every squid he tried for, but before I went to bed he had caught seven of the strange, big-eyed beasts.

It seemed a shame to waste them so the next day Claire cooked a Bay of Spirits dinner. It consisted of grilled trout followed by roast squid stuffed with minced clams, accompanied by tiny, sweet, wild peas. For dessert there were deep bowls of wild raspberries. That there was a shortage of supermarkets in Bay d'Espoir was a matter of no concern to us.

In September the question arose of where we would winter. Claire, who can be as adamant as *Happy Adventure*, refused to consider wintering in the bay. It was not that she didn't like the place but, as she pointed out:

"If we keep retrogressing every year we'll end up back at Muddy Hole; and how would you like that!"

The point was well taken. Furthermore, both Claire and I had become fond of our little house in Burgeo, and of the people of Messers Cove, and we felt it would be no hardship to spend another year there. I put the matter to *Happy Adventure* on the basis of a mutual compromise. I explained to her that we would not make any attempt to take her west of Burgeo ("this year," I added, under my breath) if she would just agree to return to Messers Cove.

However she remained suspicious of my motives, and distinctly unco-operative. After two false starts (during which we did not even get as far as Pushthrough) I put Claire on the coastal steamer for Burgeo and sent an urgent s.o.s. to Jack McClelland. Jack, ever loyal, flew to Gander, chartered a float plane, and joined me. Then he proceeded to bring *Happy Adventure* to heel. Jack can be a driver when his dander is up, taking no account of risks to life and limb. He made it very clear to the little schooner that she was either going to go to Burgeo, or she was going to go to the bottom of the sea in deep, deep water from whose icy embrace she could never again hope to emerge. I don't know how *she* felt about his do-or-die attitude, but he scared the living daylights out of me! We took risks that I don't like to think about even in retrospect, and in the end we beat our way into Messers Cove, all three of us looking as if we had engaged in the battle of the century.

It was a small victory, and it was not indicative of the way things would go in future.

During the succeeding four summers, *Happy Adventure* held me to a stalemate. My cry was "Westward Ho!" – and hers was, "Westward No!" She would go east like a lamb, but west she would not go under any circumstances. After the second summer we all but gave up trying. We gradually settled into Burgeo ways and became, perforce, real outport residents. Memories of the mainland began to dim. We forgot how and why we had come to Burgeo in the first place. We three sailed *Happy Adventure* along the coast – to the eastward – exploring the mighty fiords that split the rock face of that iron-bound seaboard. I even went so far as to build a slip at Messers upon which the schooner could be hauled each winter. She, and we, were putting down roots. She gave us almost no trouble during these years. She did not sink a single time, and her leaks and other crotchets remained manageable. She was apparently content and, it must be admitted, so were we – until the spring of 1967.

18 · *Good-bye Messers*

D URING the late winter of 1967 rumours began to reach Burgeo that Canada was celebrating her Centennial; the anniversary of the Act of Confederation which made a nation out of the northern British colonies of North America. Most residents of Burgeo found these rumours quite perplexing. As far as they were concerned, Confederation took place in 1949 when Canada was belatedly admitted into union with Newfoundland. As Uncle Dorman Collier, an elder of the village, explained to a group of men gathered in his fish store one afternoon: "A cen-teen-ial is supposed to be one hunnert year. 1949 to 1967 be more like sixteen year. Anyway 'tis nowhere nigh a hunnert. They fellows on the mainland must be some short on larnin'."

Nobody got very excited about the Centennial, but it was different when Burgeo heard about Expo 67 which, if the reports were to be believed, was going to be the biggest blowout Canada had ever had. Everyone was going to be there. All the major nations were going to build pavilions. Countries like New England, Cuba, Texas, Quebec, and Mali were all going to have their own pavilions. It was these pavilions that caught the interest of the people of Burgeo.

No one knew what a pavilion was until Dorman took it on himself to find out. He looked it up in an ornate calf-bound

dictionary that had been brought to Burgeo by Captain Elisha Fudge on his return from a voyage to Portugal with salt cod in 1867. Dorman had inherited this dictionary and he made good use of it, despite the fact that it was printed in Portuguese and Dorman did not know any Portuguese. The way he solved this problem was to make a list of all the words he wanted to look up and then wait for the arrival of a Portuguese dragger, two or three of which called at Burgeo every year for emergency supplies. When one arrived, Dorman would carry his list and dictionary on board and find a member of the crew who could translate for him.

The first Portuguese dragger of the year put in to Burgeo on May twenty-eighth. She was the *Santa Jorge*, fifteen weeks out of Lisbon, and about thirteen weeks out of alcoholic stimulants. When Dorman boarded her with his book and a bottle of contraband alky, he was royally received.

I met him a few days later at the Cottage Hospital. He said he had found out what a pavilion was, but he couldn't tell me right then because he didn't think it was "fitten" for the ears of the nurses. He said he would write it out for me and send it to Messers in a sealed envelope.

He was as good as his word.

> *Dear Skipper Mowat.*
> *A pavilion is a sort of a tilt, like a tent only bigger.*
> *Mostly it is made of canvas and silk with pictures*

painted onto it. It was built by Kings mainly in lonely
spots where nobody would know what was going on
into it. I would not tell you what was going on into
it but I guess you can guess Ha Ha Ha.

> Yrs respectfully,
> Dorman.

When this explanation of what a pavilion was percolated around the village it generated a mass movement to attend Expo. The two ministers were against it, and so was the majority of the women. Madge Kearley was in favour. Madge was what you might call a working spinstress. She had worked hard all her life and didn't have much to show for it except thirteen children. Madge said that a bunch of kings would be a nice change from a bunch of Portuguese sailors who had been out from Lisbon fifteen weeks. Madge said she was going to go to Expo if she had to swim and if she missed any pavilions it wouldn't be for want of trying.

The excitement about Expo had its unsettling effect upon almost everyone in Burgeo, and Claire and I and Albert were not immune. We talked about it and one evening Claire suggested that we try to sail *Happy Adventure* to Expo. When I laughed hollowly, she replied:

"No, Farley. I really mean it. There'll never be a better time to go."

I knew what she meant.

In February an incident had occurred which had ruptured the even tenor of our Burgeo ways. A female fin whale weighing about eighty tons, and heavy with calf, had become trapped in a salt-water pond near the settlement. Here she provided an irresistible target for the guns of a handful of Burgeo men until I interceded and stopped the shooting. Unhappily it stopped too late. The whale died from the wounds she received and the press, radio, and television across much of North America thereupon unleashed a barrage of contumely upon the whole of Burgeo. The bewildered residents were at first stunned by this attention from a world they did not know; and then became bitterly resentful. As was to be expected, much of the resentment was focused on me, and it was demonstrated in no uncertain manner when the rotting body of the monster was towed to a little harbour adjacent to my house (shades of Pushthrough), and left there, presumably as a suggestion that I mind my own business in future.

By the end of May the dead whale was only poisoning the atmosphere in the harbour proper, but I knew what to expect during the hot summer months, when eighty tons of meat and blubber would begin to decompose in earnest.

It did indeed seem like an appropriate time for us to depart from Burgeo.

The problem was how to persuade *Happy Adventure* to agree. One day I received a press release describing how the seafaring heritage of the Atlantic provinces was to be represented at Expo by a replica of the famous Nova Scotian schooner, *Bluenose*. Now Newfoundland and Nova Scotian schooners have always been arch rivals. I took the release down to the slip where *Happy Adventure* drowsed and I read it to her, not once but three times, and slowly, to make sure she understood. And then I ruminated aloud about this intolerable affront to all Newfoundland vessels. Finally I suggested that the situation could be remedied if we voyaged to Expo ourselves.

"We'll show them," I said cheerfully as I slapped her buttocks, "won't we, old girl?"

If she understood, she gave no sign. I could only hope I had gotten through.

We kept her on her slip while we prepared her for a voyage of just over fourteen hundred nautical miles. I hired Dolph Moulton, who was a sound shipwright, to help me put her in shape and the two of us, assisted at sundry times by every able-bodied man in Messers, laboured over her as few ships have ever been laboured over.

We left nothing to chance. We hawsed out all her seams and recaulked them. We stripped off and replaced every plank that seemed the least bit dubious. Then we coated the entire hull with a space-age epoxy glue, bedded canvas into it, applied another layer of epoxy, and gave the whole vessel a second layer of brand-new, one-inch, pine planking. We caulked this new outer planking, and applied three coats of copper paint below the water line and four coats of black paint above it. When we finished, the hull was about three inches thick and so strong the little vessel could probably have been dropped by a crane without spraining a rib.

There was no way she could leak. Nevertheless I played it safe. One Saturday I hired a score of little boys with buckets to fill her up with sea water while she stood on the slip. The job took them all day. In the evening Dolph and I and Uncle

Josh and Uncle Art and a dozen other men sat around under her hull and watched for drips. Not one drop came through.

The satisfaction we felt was expressed admirably by Dolph.

"Tight me son? She's tight as a maiden's drum!"

She seemed tight all right, but I had been fooled so many times before that I was taking no chances. I had sent for, and we had installed two brand new pumps. One was a modern impeller pump of fabulous capacity, driven by a belt from the engine. Even if, by some freak of devilishness, she did manage to leak a little, I would be able to circumvent her suicidal tendencies.

We launched her off the following evening at high tide. She took the water sweetly and bobbed out to her mooring, where she lay lightly on the harbour looking as pretty as a tickle-ass (the local name for a kind of gull). When I rowed out to check her at ten o'clock there was no more than a pailful of water in her bilges. I went to bed that night to a sound sleep, confident that *Happy Adventure* would sink no more.

I was awakened early the following morning. Dorman Collier's charming daughter was standing in our kitchen making throat-clearing noises. Sleepily I pulled on my trousers and came out to see what she wanted.

"Oh, Mr. Mowat," she said, and there was a catch in her voice that showed she was close to tears, "Father says you'd best come quick. '*Appy Hadventure*'s going down."

From the kitchen window I could see my little ship. I could see her masts, her red-painted cabin trunk – and about six inches of her hull. Several dories surrounded her and her deck was alive with men and boys armed with pails, dancing a wild fandango. A curtain of flung water hung prettily about her.

By noon we had bailed her out to the bottom of the engine which we drained and refilled with oil. Being a good English diesel it started without trouble and the impeller pump took over, sending a fire-hose stream across the harbour. *Happy Adventure* had been foiled again – but only for the moment. It was now all too clear what her answer was to my hopeful suggestion that she might be willing to make the voyage to Expo 67.

We hauled her again, and went over her so carefully that I believe we actually checked every single nail hole. We found no indication of where the water was getting in. Completely baffled, Dolph suggested that we launch her off, stand pump watch on her, and wait for her to "take up" – and at those words a memory came surging through my mind. I remembered Enos Coffin standing on the end of the stage at Muddy Hole:

"Southern Shore boats all leaks a drop when they first lanches off ... but once they been afloat awhile, why they takes up ...."

We launched her off, and she took up the whole of Messers Cove during a ten-day period, and we pumped it all out of her again. By the end of two weeks we had begun to wear her down. The leaks grew smaller until, by the end of the month that it took to complete preparations for the trip, she was only leaking her normal fifty gallons a day.

Reactions to our proposed voyage varied considerably. The Newfoundland Establishment, which had found me something of a thorn in its side both at the municipal and at the provincial level, sent me encouraging messages of which this one is typical:

OVERJOYED HEAR YOUR PLANS STOP MY GOVERNMENT ANX-
IOUS ASSIST ANY POSSIBLE WAY EXPEDITE YOUR DEPARTURE
THE ONLY LIVING FATHER

The signature was a playful allusion to the fact that, as a result of Newfoundland's late entry into Canada, Premier Joey Smallwood was indeed the only surviving Father of Confederation. The rest of them, including my own great-great uncle Oliver Mowat, had been decently buried for seventy years or more.

On the other hand my real friends were appalled at my intentions. Jack McClelland, who had long since concluded that *Happy Adventure* was little more than a floating coffin, sent me a wire which (although I did not know it for some months) orginated as:

DONT BE AN ASS YOU ARE A SILLY BASTARD

but which reached me as:

DONT BE AN ASP YOU ARE A FRILLY BUSTARD

This wire gave me much food for thought, as I tried to puzzle out what difference it would make to Jack if I became a poisonous Egyptian reptile instead of remaining an Arabian game-bird.

When Jack found he could not change my mind, he made a heroic gesture. On the next steamer I received a crate from him which contained:

4 inflatable life vests complete with shark-repellent packs;

1 emergency shortwave radio of the Mae West type without any power tube;

1 case of distress rockets;

1 inflatable rubber lifeboat, certified by the British Board of Trade to carry twenty-five people.

This shipment was accompanied by a letter informing me that Jack intended to protect his investment in the boat, and in me, by personally accompanying *Happy Adventure* through the more dangerous stretches between Burgeo and Montreal.

The mere idea of this filled me with horror. The odds against our survival were, God knows, already about as heavy as they could be. Claire and Albert shared my concern, and both of them made it clear that the moment Jack stepped aboard was going to be the moment they stepped ashore.

By the time we moved aboard *Happy Adventure* on August first, my confidence in the whole venture had been severely eroded. What, two months earlier, had appeared to be the prospect of a pleasant voyage to Expo now loomed as an ordeal from which it seemed unlikely that any of us would emerge unscathed. My one remaining hope was that the weather, which had been atrocious since late May, would stay that way until October, giving me at least a semi-legitimate excuse for remaining snugly moored in Messers Cove until the whole idiotic scheme had been forgotten. The weather on the Sou'west Coast being what it was, I felt reasonably safe in publicly announcing that we would sail on the first fair-weather day.

Wednesday, August second, dawned fair. For the first time in three weeks there was no fog, although the edge of the bank that lives perpetually on the Sou'west Coast still lurked a few miles away. At 0700 hours, when I apprehensively stuck my head out the companion hatch (hoping against hope to find it a foul day) there were no fewer than fifty people of all ages lining the hills around Messers Cove.

South Coast Newfoundlanders are generally undemonstrative. The audience that almost circled the harbour was a quiet one, and patient. Nevertheless I was acutely aware of them. I could sense that they were waiting for something. Claire joined me in the companionway and after a brief look about her, she said:

"Well, I suppose we have to go. We don't want to disappoint the audience."

I said: "Yes. Well. I suppose we had. But first I think I'd better check the engine bedding bolts again . . . and I have to lay out my chart courses . . . and I'd better take Albert ashore for a run because it may be a long time before he gets another chance . . . and. . . ."

I did all these things, and many more, but it was no good. The wind did not change. The fog did not roll back to cloak my blue funk in a comforting anonymity. The patient watchers on the shore did not go off about their business.

At 1400 hours I took a surreptitious drink from the bottle I kept handy in the engine room, poured a dollop over the side (breathing a heartfelt prayer at the same time) and tried to start the engine. The damned thing started like a shot. No further scope for evasive manoeuvres remained to me.

"All right!" I cried in a ringing falsetto voice to my crew. "Stand by . . . let go the moorings!"

Claire trundled forward, slipped the heavy bridle off the niggerheads and flung it overboard. I pushed in the gear lever. The engine thundered and the big propeller kicked a gush of water under the stern. *Happy Adventure* was under way.

The people on shore got to their feet and some of the younger ones began waving. Frank Harvey stood on the end of his stage with a conch horn and blew a lugubrious salute.

For thirty seconds I felt the exhilaration that comes to every sailor, no matter how timid he may be, when he finally severs the umbilical cord that binds him to the land.

Then there was a hell of a jolt! It pitched Albert clean over the bows into the water. It nearly broke both my shins against the cockpit combing. It flung Claire against the main-mast. And it brought *Happy Adventure* to a dead stop.

The engine stalled, and there we were, utterly motionless, part of a silent tableau which seemed frozen into time-less immobility. It was as if some giant, unseen hand had reached out to stay us in our passing. Actually, though, it was the umbilical cord.

Our permanent mooring was designed to hold a large steamer during hurricane weather. A thousand-pound block of cement sunk in the bottom ooze was connected to the mooring buoy by a massive chain. Attached to the buoy was a bridle made of three-inch-diameter nylon rope. Now, I had forgotten that nylon floats – and had steamed right over the floating bridle. The propeller had picked it up and wound it tightly around the shaft.

Sim Spencer, my closest Burgeo friend, got into his dory and rowed out to us. Together we hung over the dory's gun-wale and stared down at the serpentine mess of black-and-yellow rope wound around the shaft. Sim shook his head.

"We'll have to unshackle the buoy and haul the vessel back out on the slip to clear her, Skipper," he said sadly.

Half an hour earlier I would have thought those were the sweetest words I had ever heard. Not now. It may have been shame, rage, or perhaps something more profound; something that even the most timid sailor may occasionally be privileged to feel: the realization that no real seafaring man ever really masters his fear – he only learns to live with it.

"I'll be goddamned if I will!" I cried and, stripping off my clothes, I took my sheath knife in my teeth and plunged overboard.

This may not sound like much, but to the Burgeo people it was an electrifying act. They do not swim. There is little point in their learning the art because the sea thereabouts seldom grows as warm as thirty-eight degrees, and a man can only endure exposure to such a water temperature for a few minutes. When the watchers saw me plunge, stark naked, into those chill depths they believed I was gone for good.

I nearly was. The shock was so great I immediately lost my breath. I surfaced and was hauled back into the dory by a really anxious Sim who implored me not to try again.

Being already numb, the shock of my second plunge was not so severe, and I got down to the propeller and had begun to saw at the thick rope when Albert joined me. He nosed me aside and began to worry the rope with his teeth. I surfaced and was again hauled aboard the dory. I was ready to give up, but Claire leaned over *Happy Adventure*'s stern and in her hand was a glass full of rum.

"If you're determined to commit suicide," she said gently, "you might as well die happy."

I went down three more times before the rope was severed. Albert went down at least twice as often and whether the credit should go to him or to me remains a moot question. He is a modest dog and seldom makes claims on his own behalf.

Happy Adventure was now free – and drifting rapidly down on Messers Island, a scant fifty yards away. Not stopping to dress I sprang to the engine, started it, and rammed it into reverse. Nothing happened. We continued to drift down upon the rocks. Bounding forward like a naked ape I let go the main anchor. The vessel brought up, swung, and came to rest with her stern so close to the rocks that Albert, who was still fooling about in the water, climbed a boulder and jumped aboard. He may have thought the whole ma-noeuvre was for his benefit.

This was finally too much for the stolidity of the audi-ence. Among them all, I suppose, they had witnessed ten thousand vessel departures – but they had never witnessed one like this. Everyone who could reach a boat piled into one and in a few minutes the harbour was alive with dories, skiffs, and trap boats. They clustered around *Happy Adven-ture* like burying beetles around a putative corpse.

Several men explained to me, all at once, what the matter was. The shock of the sudden stop had jerked the propeller shaft out of the sleeve that connected it to the engine. The vessel (this was the unanimous opinion) would now *have* to go on the slip to be repaired.

But they reckoned without the spirit which, however briefly, still possessed me. Clad only in my underwear shorts (and I would not have been clad in those had not Claire in-sisted) I jumped into Sim's dory, grabbed an oar, thrust it between the sternpost and the propeller, and began to lever with all my strength.

The oar snapped, and I savagely grabbed another. The clustered boats began to back away and there was an uneasy silence. The blade of the second oar split and pieces came floating to the surface. Uncle Bert Hahn, in the nearest dory, must have sensed what was going to happen next. He made a frantic attempt to back clear, but I leaned over Sim's gun-wale and snatched an oar right out of his hand. It was a good oar, one that he had made himself, and while Sim held his dory in position I slowly levered the shaft forward and into its sleeve again.

It took me only a few more minutes to tighten the set screws on the sleeve, restart the engine, and test the gears. This time the propeller turned as it should.

"Get up the goddamned anchor!" I shrilled at my crew. Almost before it had broken clear of the bottom I shoved the throttle full ahead, executed a turn that made *Happy Adven-*

ture spin like a giddy girl, and we went rumbling off toward the harbour entrance, scattering little boats before us like herring.

I did not look back. When a man has made a really monumental asp of himself, he should never, never look back.

19· *The alien shore*

ALTHOUGH the sky was clear, there was a strong west wind and before we emerged from the shelter of the Burgeo Islands we were having a hard buck. Wind and sea grew steadily worse and *Happy Adventure* began to leak. She was soon taking twenty gallons an hour and was evidently determined to keep it all because the pumps plugged up, having again become choked with sludge that was being washed around in the bilges by the little vessel's athletic leaps and bounds. While Claire steered, I struggled with the pumps but I could not keep them clear.

It began to look as if *Happy Adventure* had won again. However, an alternative to turning tail and fleeing ignominiously back to Burgeo still remained. Close in under the shore cliffs a maze of reefs and sunkers formed an inside passage that offered some protection from the seas, while at the same time threatening to skewer any vessel that dared to enter the dubious shelter of its breakers.

Had I not made such a mess of our departure, I might have taken the sensible course and returned to Burgeo, but this was more than I could face; better the sunkers and the reefs. I headed in for the lee of land.

Neither Claire nor Albert were sufficiently experienced to be aware of the risks to which I was exposing them as we began to pick our way through the labyrinth of foaming water and naked rock. While Albert contentedly sniffed the land smells, Claire waxed poetic.

"My," she said admiringly, "how lovely those breakers are, sending the spray over the rocks just like bridal veils." That was a woman's point of view. To me the great gouts of foaming spray towering all around us looked more like winding sheets.

Now *Happy Adventure* played her trump card. The engine began to race and the vessel stopped answering her helm. When I scrambled below I found that the propeller shaft had slipped out of its sleeve again. Only a quarter of an inch of shaft still protruded through the stuffing box into the boat. This was just enough to allow me to get a precarious hold on it with a monkey wrench and slowly twist it inboard until I could reconnect it. By the time I got back on deck we were drifting onto a particularly pretty sunker, all covered with bridal veils.

As we zigzagged in the precarious lee of the reefs I was able to clear the pump intakes but by the time we came abeam of Grand Bruit, the first settlement west of Burgeo, I had had enough. We headed in.

I was in a depressed and gloomy state of mind for I was thinking bleakly of the morrow, and of all the other morrows that stretched westward toward Montreal. Claire and Albert, on the other hand, were full of gaiety. Grand Bruit is a tiny place, but spectacularly lovely. Furthermore, its handful of inhabitants are the most hospitable people in all of Newfoundland. Half of them were on hand to take our lines, and the other half soon appeared bearing gifts ranging from a fresh-caught salmon to a jar of partridge-berry jam. Claire was entranced.

Albert was too. This was his natal place, and almost the

last place in the world where his ancient race still survived. He celebrated his return by leaping out on the dock and being rude to five of his brothers and sisters (some may have been his uncles and aunts), thus precipitating a dogfight that was terminated only when a half dozen men armed with shovels whacked and pushed the whole howling, squalling mass into the harbour – from which the dogs emerged as friends and comrades, all enmity forgotten.

Although I had secretly concluded that this was where the voyage to Expo was going to end, I told nobody of my decision. I wanted time to prepare my crew for the news that they would be spending the next several years in Grand Bruit. I devoted most of that night to aligning and tightening the shaft sleeve and repacking the stuffing box which had been responsible for much of the leakage. When I finally climbed into my bunk the pre-dawn sky had become overcast, the wind had swung southerly, and I knew that summer (both days of it) on the Sou'west Coast was, thank God, at an end. It was going to blow like the devil in the morning and the fog would be impenetrable. I slept easy in the knowledge that the ordeal was over, that there was no way this ill-starred voyage was going to continue any farther.

I can offer no reasonable explanation for what actually happened the next day. The inexplicable facts are these: when I woke at nine o'clock it was to find a clear, cloudless day, not a breath of wind, perfect visibility, and a sea as calm as an average lily pond. And *Happy Adventure* was not leaking. At first I did not believe any of it, but when conditions had not changed by noon I had to accept the unpalatable conclusion that there was nothing, short of my sabotaging the boat or engine, that was going to enable me to abandon the voyage. Although I was convinced that I was being made the victim of a terrible trick, I was helpless to do anything about it. With most of the population of Grand Bruit gathered on the wharf to wish us Godspeed (and patently wondering what was delaying our departure), I was forced against the pull of every fibre of my being to go to sea once more.

What followed was one of the worst days of my life. The fantastic weather conditions (a day like this comes once in a decade on the Sou'west Coast) continued hour after hour. Nothing went wrong with the engine. The leaks did not re-appear. We steamed along a sunlit, smiling coast over a glinting, mirror sea. And all the time I knew something *had* to happen and I had to be ready for it. I was so keyed-up by the certainty that we were being fattened like lambs for a sudden slaughter that I snapped at Claire, cursed my poor little boat, snarled at Albert, and was generally obnoxious.

Years later when I described that day to a friend in St. John's, he advanced a rather singular explanation.

"Farley," he said, "I don't think you had any idea how anxious Joey Smallwood was to get you off his island. And if The Only Living Father can successfully bamboozle half a million people for twenty years, he must have access to powers we can't even envision."

Late that night we steamed into Port aux Basques harbour after a completely uneventful cruise that would have been child's play for three men in a tub. We had arrived at our point of ultimate departure from the island of Newfoundland.

The ease with which we reached Port aux Basques did not make me overconfident about the future. On the contrary, I became more and more convinced that *Happy Adventure* was only biding her time, trying to put me off guard. I could not believe that after all those years of successfully thwarting my design to take her west she was now going to submit so tamely.

The Cabot Strait separating Newfoundland and Nova Scotia is ninety miles wide. It is notorious for the bad weather it breeds, and for the heavy currents which combine with an ever-present swell to build up a wicked sea. I knew Claire and Albert were not yet up to such a challenge so I had arranged for Capt. John Parker, Master Mariner in sail and

steam, and at that time Chief Pilot for North Sydney, to join me in Port aux Basques. John arrived from North Sydney on the big ferry, *William Carson*, early the next morning. I took Claire and Albert down to the *Carson* and put them in the charge of her skipper, big, affable Capt. Charlie Brown.

Charlie gave them his own comfortable quarters, then took all of us to the bridge to hear the latest weather report. It was not good. It called for strong sou'east winds, bad visibility, thunder squalls and heavy rain.

"Hmm," said Charlie. "Going to be an uncomfortable crossing on the *Carson*. Course, it won't bother you fellows, snug in harbour here. It should blow out in a couple of days, then you can make a dart across."

At noon the whistle blew to signal the big ship's departure. John and I said our good-byes and went ashore. As we made our way back to the harbour John horrified me by saying:

"Well, I guess we'd better get under way about two o'clock this afternoon. That'll mean we'll raise Cape Breton in daylight tomorrow morning."

"Good God! John! You have to be kidding! Didn't you *hear* the weather, and what Charlie said?"

John, who is small of stature, lean, and taut as whipcord, and apparently afraid of nothing on this earth, shrugged and replied:

"Oh, that. Well, Farley, if you wait for good weather in

the Strait you'll wait a lifetime. We'd better take what's going and make the best of it."

Who was I to argue with a man who had been skipper of a three-masted schooner, sailing to South America, at a time when I was still paddling a canoe upon the sylvan waters of Ontario streams?

We went aboard and John looked over *Happy Adventure*. He seemed satisfied with her – except for one thing.

"Where's your radar reflector?"

I admitted to not having one of those triangular metal devices which give off a strong reflection, enabling radar-equipped ships to pick you up on their scopes and steer clear of you.

"We better get one," John said. "Most of the seaway traffic is using the Strait right now. Lots of big ships. We'll be crossing right through them, in thick weather."

I was only too willing, but in all of Port aux Basques there was not such an animal to be had for love or money. In the end we lashed a ten-gallon pail in the port shrouds. It looked a little odd, but John seemed to think it would do the trick.

We put out on schedule at 1400 hours, and I did not like the look of things at all. A big, oily swell – the sure precursor of a blow – was rolling in from sou'east. The sky was overcast and ominously murky. If someone had written STORM in thousand-foot letters across the rolling clouds, the omens could not have been any clearer. I glanced at John, but he was calm and relaxed, sucking on his pipe as he held the tiller, and no doubt cogitating about the contents of a book he was writing about schooner days. As unobtrusively as possible I went below to the engine room.

We punched out to sea and the mountains of the Long Range grew dim and disappeared from view astern. The swell grew worse until *Happy Adventure* was pitching like a demented thing. The leaks saw their chance and opened up – and once again the guck in the bilge began to put the pumps out of action.

By ten o'clock it was pitch dark. The wind was rising, as predicted, and the combination of wind-lop and heavy swell produced a motion that was indescribable. I hope John will forgive me, but I can only do justice to that motion by reporting that when John went below to try and get a nap, he was immediately sick. He was violently sick – and he had been going to sea, both man and boy, for thirty years! The only reason I did not follow his example was that I was too terrified.

By this time we had given up trying to make a course for Sydney. We came around on the other tack and tried to run to the westward toward the lonely island of St. Paul, behind whose rocky cliffs we hoped we might find a lee if the storm grew worse.

The storm grew worse. The six-thousand-ton ferry, *Leif Eriksson*, passed close to starboard of us, inbound for Port aux Basques, and we began to realize what we were up against by the way *she* was pitching into it, heaving great broken seas clean over her massive bows.

By midnight we had very little idea where we were. We were shipping it green right over the whole boat so that chart work was impossible. Our oil navigation lights had blown out and we could not get forward to relight them. We were a tiny black vessel on a black sea in a black night, invisible to the human eye, and we had to put all our trust in that ten-gallon pail lashed in the shrouds. The trust was not misplaced. Although we never saw her, the *Patrick Morris*, a rail ferry, picked us up on radar from ten miles away. Unable to make out who we were, or what the devil we were doing, her skipper took no chances, and swung his big ship away off course to give us plenty of sea room. Presumably other vessels did the same, for we saw no sign of any living thing until the dawn.

Dawn was an interminable time in coming. The wind rose to gusts of fifty miles an hour. The jib halyard parted, leaving us under foresail alone. The exhaust pipe snapped off from the skin fitting that led it through the hull, not only filling the engine room with fumes, but allowing the Cabot Strait to spew into the boat through a two-inch diameter hole whenever we rolled the starboard rail down. As a result of this mishap we had to come over to the port tack and stay there, hoping we would not run square into the towering, nine-hundred-foot headland of Cape North.

We had given up all hope of finding St. Paul, and were simply trying to stay alive somewhere in mid-Strait and ride out the storm as best we could. The confused sea grew so heavy that it washed the name boards off the schooner's bows, and we were being swept from end to end. The leaks grew steadily worse, and kept me pumping forty minutes of every hour using the hand pump, while the engine-driven pump ran continuously. Luckily, most of the guck seemed to have gone overboard and the pump suctions remained fairly free.

At daybreak, in heavy rain and thunder squalls, the wind shifted to west-southwest and we raised the loom of distant land. This had to be the highlands of Cape North, so we decided to run in under the cliffs and make for the little harbour of Dingwall, or perhaps Ingonish. But as we crawled closer to the land we could see immense breakers roaring white in the mouths of both harbours, effectively barring all possibility of entry.

There was then nothing for it but to work south along a thundering weather shore, in the hopes of getting into the entrance to the Bras d'Or Lakes – a complex of great salt-water lakes that fills the interior of Cape Breton Island. John kept the helm while I now pumped continuously. When we hauled the patent log I found we had covered a hundred and twenty miles through the water, much of this distance in the wrong direction.

But all things end. As the sun rose, breaking through the scudding clouds, the wind began to fall off. By noon the storm was over. The seas and swell flattened out and I even managed to find time from pumping to cook some food, the first we had tasted since the voyage began. The day brightened and grew warm and at six o'clock that evening we swung around Bird Island and entered the long, smooth, summer-sleeping gut leading into the heart of the great island of Cape Breton. Shortly thereafter we docked at a lobster fisherman's wharf. After thirty hours of struggle, *Happy Adventure* had finally been parted from her native land to become a stranger on an alien shore.

Claire and Albert were surprised to see us when the lobster fisherman drove us into North Sydney late that evening. The *Carson* had had a rough trip as predicted, and Charlie Brown had assured them we would not get out of Port aux Basques for a week at least. But Charlie Brown did not know John Parker as I now knew him. I am not sure I would want to go pleasure cruising with John, but if I ever again have to make a hard passage under dangerous conditions, *he* is the man I want beside me.

The next day Claire and I and Albert took *Happy Adventure* on into the lakes, to the calm and gentle little backwater of Baddeck where there was a small shipyard run by the Pinaud family. Here we intended to haul *Happy Adventure* out, and *keep* hauling her out, until her leaks were cured once and for all.

She gave no trouble on this passage. She may have been too exhausted, but I think it more likely she was suffering from culture shock. The contrast between her native land and these green and pleasant shores, with their lush and prosperous farms running down to lethargic waters; the summer heat, foglessness and galelessness seemed, taken together, to befuddle her to the point where she was as amiable as a cut cat.

When we entered the picture-book harbour at Baddeck the basin was crowded with gorgeously accoutred yachts, glistening with polished brass and chrome and manned and womaned by gleaming paragons of fashion. Surrounded by all this conspicuous consumption, even Claire and I felt out of place – as for *Happy Adventure*, the effect must have been shattering. She could not have failed to realize how uncouth and dowdy she appeared in comparison to these floating pleasure palaces and, like any country girl suddenly exposed to the contemptuous stare of high society, she got that sinking feeling.

No sooner did we come alongside the dock than she opened up as if the bottom had fallen out of her. Only prompt action by Fred and Ralph Pinaud, who dashed to the rescue with a battery of electric pumps, prevented her from burying her shame at the bottom of the harbour.

Albert, on the other hand, was not the least bit discountenanced by this new world. He celebrated his arrival by going ashore and jumping a huge, dull-eyed, blue poodle off one of the yachts. In its simple-minded arrogance the poodle thought to dispute passageway with him. Albert did not deign to fight: he just caught the poodle by one floppy ear, swung it with a shake of his massive shoulders, dumped it into the harbour, then went on his way with not a glance behind. By that action he endeared himself to all the boatyard workers, and they made much of him for the remainder of our stay.

The next morning the Pinauds hauled the schooner and

four of us spent a full day working on her. As usual we could find no apparent cause for the leakage so we recaulked her, applied sheet lead to the angle between her garbuts and her keel, slathered paint on her, and launched her off.

She immediately began to leak almost as badly as before she was hauled out. This infuriated the Pinaud brothers who yanked her out of the water again. This time *six* men went over her as with a fine-tooth comb. They found nothing new. In desperation they put in a new set of stopwaters. Then we launched her for the second time.

That evening she lay at the wharf – and she did not leak. This was cause for a celebration – but it was premature. At midnight, as he was about to leave us, Ralph Pinaud casually glanced into my little vessel's bilges. His roar of rage must have been audible over most of Cape Breton. The bilges were full. The water was already lapping over the engine room floorboards.

We put the electric pumps to work, and went to sleep.

In the morning Ralph came back aboard.

"There's no use hauling this – – – – – boat again," he told us. "There is just one hope for her, just one. See that mud bank on the other side of the basin? Yes? Well, you put your engine full astern and you run this something-basket of yours right onto that mud bank as hard as you damn well can!"

"And leave her there? And take a train to Expo?" I asked hopefully.

"No, Sir! You don't leave her in *my* basin. When she's hard aground you keep your engine turning over in reverse. Let her propeller stir up all the mud it can. Stay there for six hours and then we'll haul you off . . . and see."

I was not about to argue with Ralph, who had the look about him of a man close to the end of his tether. Meekly I obeyed instructions. We backed *Happy Adventure* full tilt on to the mud bank, and there she stayed all day, churning away and gradually oozing herself backward into the soft shoreline like a turtle digging a nest.

Late in the afternoon an incredibly elaborate yacht

motored into the basin. She outglittered all the others. Her name (and I am *not* making this up) was *Patrician*. Her crew and owner wore sweaters with the name emblazoned across them in gold letters. She came from Ohio, and it was clear from her attitude that she was slumming. As she manoeuvred toward the wharf she came close to us, and her portly owner (one could hardly feel justified in calling him skipper) hailed me and asked in a condescending sort of a way if I wanted a tow.

I said no, thanks. I said that my boat was on the mud because that was where I wanted her to be. I asked him if he had ever heard of Ohio women using mud packs to improve their faces? When he nodded, I explained that it was customary in Nova Scotia to use the same treatment on our boats–to improve their bottoms. And then I suggested he might personally benefit from the same treatment himself. His subsequent landing at the wharf was not the best I have seen, but he may have had something on his mind.

After dinner that evening we pulled *Happy Adventure* off her muddy couch and brought her back to the wharf. Ralph and Fred stayed with us all that evening, peering into the bilges every few minutes. And, miracle of miracles, she did not leak. Not then, and not that night, and not the next day.

"She sucked the mud right into her," Ralph explained. "Filled her pores right up with mud. Now she can't leak no matter how she tries . . . not until the mud washes out of her, that is. And when it does, well, you better find yourself another mud bank, quick."

Ralph Pinaud is one of the few true geniuses left upon this earth.

20· *Hello Expo!*

I<small>T WAS</small> well into August before *Happy Adventure* was ready to sail. By then we had all had our fill of rich men's yachts. Not that Baddeck contained nothing else. Something of the curse was taken off the gilded flotilla by the presence of several real boatmen. There was Dr. Paul Sheldon from New York, then in his seventies, who each year sailed his stout old sloop around Newfoundland and even down the Labrador coast. There was Bob Carr, who had built a perfect replica of Capt. Joshua Slocum's famous *Spray*, and then sailed her to the West Indies and back. And there was Rory, an Irish gynaecologist, preparing to sail his vessel across the Atlantic in a bid to escape for a few months from women's woes.

Baddeck was not so bad if you chose the company you kept, but Claire and I were anxiously eyeing the calendar and wondering if this voyage too would abort far short of its intended destination. Time was fast running on, but we were not.

We left Baddeck at noon on the twelfth, and made an unreal passage through the misty lochs of Bras d'Or to St. Peters canal. Clear of the canal we swung west through Lennox Passage which separates Isle Madame from Cape Breton Island.

Isle Madame was settled long ago by French-speaking

Acadians and is linked to Cape Breton proper by a causeway and an antique swing-bridge. The bridge is operated by horse-power. The horse lives on the Isle Madame side, and he is an Acadian horse. He does not take kindly to the modern world of hurry and flurry.

Paul Sheldon had told me about this horse and warned me not to approach him in an imperious spirit. Be polite to him, Paul said, and be prepared to take your time.

We followed Paul's advice. Coming abeam of the farm where the horse lived (it lay a mile east of the bridge) we blew three gentle toots on our hand fog-horn, and then anchored while Claire set about preparing lunch. It was a lovely sunny day and we sat and drowsed over a bottle of wine, occasionally glancing up at the distant farm buildings.

The horse was not home when we arrived. He was away at a neighbour's farm helping with the harvest, but in mid-afternoon he appeared and ambled down toward the bridge. He was half-way there before his human partner, the nominal bridgemaster, appeared from the farmhouse and began to follow after.

At this juncture there came a swelling roar from the eastward and a few minutes later a huge power cruiser thundered into view making about twenty knots. She passed us without slowing down, and her wake not only upset my glass of wine, but my temper too. My verbal broadside in her direction was drowned out by three long raucous blasts from her multiple klaxon horns. She wanted the bridge opened, and she wanted it opened *then*! She did not slow down and I had rising hopes that she might crash right into the bridge piers and sink herself, but at the last instant she went hard astern, sending up huge gouts of water and exhaust fumes. With roaring engines she began to back and fill in front of the closed span, obviously furious at being delayed.

Claire had been on the foredeck preparing to haul up our anchor when this behemoth appeared upon the scene.

"Never mind the anchor," I called to her. "Look at the horse!"

The horse had stopped in his tracks some three hundred yards short of the bridge. With ears canted forward he watched the floating gin palace going into its tantrum for a moment, then he turned sedately about and began walking back toward the farm. He and the bridgemaster passed each other, but as far as I could tell there was no overt communication between them. The man continued toward the bridge while the yacht shattered the quiet day with a second and then a third series of irate klaxon blasts.

She was then charging angrily back and forth parallel to the bridge. She slowed as the bridgemaster leaned over the railing. We were too far away to hear the conversation that ensued, but the bridgemaster gave us the gist of it later on.

"Well, Monsieur, this fellow, he tell me he is le président for some big company. He tell me to open goddamn bridge vite, because he is in big hurry. I listen till he finish then I tell him about my horse. You see, that horse, he does not like the loud noise. When he hear the loud noise he go back to his stable, and he go inside, and he stay there until whoever make that loud noise, he go away. I tell le président I am sorry but that horse he will not come back to open the bridge while that big boat she is in Lennox Passage. I tell him he must go back around outside Isle Madame and, by gar, after he swear some words like I never hear before, that is what he have to do."

We saw the yacht swing on her heel, open up her engines and come thundering back toward us, but this time I was ready. I kept my glass in my hand and didn't lose a drop. I caught a glimpse of a meaty-faced chap in a gold-braided cap on the flying bridge, hands clutching the wheel as if he would have liked to rip it right off its mounting and face so crimson that, had I been a heart specialist, I would have taken *Happy Adventure* in pursuit, with reasonable assurance of getting a job out of it.

When the last echo of the twin engines had died away the horse came out of the barn, looked searchingly up and down the passage, then strolled down to where the bridgemaster was smoking his pipe and admiring the sky. The two of them hitched themselves to a wooden beam that went around and around, and opened the bridge. As we came abeam of the open span we paused to have a little chat. The horse came over to the rail and looked down at us. He and Albert seemed to like each other and I could understand why they should find themselves *en rapport*. They must be the two most independent-minded animals that I have ever met.

For the next few days the gods were with us. *Happy Adventure's* mud pack did its work, and she herself remained remarkably docile. Possibly she had begun to take some pleasure in the novelty of this new world. We passed through the Canso Gut, and entered the curving scimitar of the Northumberland Strait, which separates mainland Nova Scotia from Prince Edward Island. Except for a brief hassle with a line squall that laid the little vessel right over on her side, and all but pitched Claire and Albert overboard, the voyage to Pictou, our next port-of-call, was without notable event.

Pictou was where Jack McClelland joined us and, true to their oath, Claire and Albert immediately went ashore.

I watched them depart with a certain wistfulness, and the secret wish that I could join them. It was not that I had anything against Jack as a shipmate; it was only that I knew he would not be happy until he got himself, and me, and *Happy Adventure*, into jeopardy.

There was bad weather forecast for that afternoon and I concluded we should wait until next morning to depart. Jack would have none of it.

"Now look," he said with his usual vehemence, "I can only spare a week to help you get this hulk to Expo. That's twelve hundred miles in seven days. We'll sail day and night. Is that understood?"

"Yes, Jack," I replied meekly.

I went ashore to cast off the moorings, and was accosted by an elderly tug-boat skipper who had been listening intently to our conversation.

"My, my, my," he said admiringly. "Now ain't that mate of yorn just *full* of piss and vinegar?"

We sailed at dusk, making straight up the centre of the Northumberland Strait. It blew a moderate breeze, and there was a good chop and some rough water when we ran into a series of tide rips, but all went reasonably well until, toward dawn, the wind dropped out and was succeeded by a heavy mist. For several hours we steamed on a compass course that should have taken us well clear of any land. But at 0800 hours, while I was below making breakfast, I was electrified by a cry from Jack.

"Land ho! And dead ahead!"

Sure enough, directly ahead of us, seen dimly through the mist, was a low shore and, between us and it, what looked like another tidal rip with waves boiling up and breaking white.

Jack argued that the land must belong to Nova Scotia and that Cape Tormentine must have extended itself out into the middle of the strait during the night. The truth was we were lost. While we discussed the matter I took another look at the "tide rip" and to my horror realized it was not a rip, but a waste of shoal water. A quick check of the chart showed it had to be the infamous Tryon Shoals which lie up against the shores of Prince Edward Island. We were miles off our proper course, and in a fair way to ending our voyage right there and then.

We clawed clear and I set a new course, but not very confidently. Our compass had obviously gone haywire and could no longer be trusted. It seemed to be off about ten degrees and the wonder is that it was not off even more, for when I looked into the compass box I found, nestled against the compass itself, a large steel screwdriver.

I never did discover for certain how it got there. Jack muttered something about having had trouble with the engine throttle, which was mounted next to the compass, during the night. That was as far as he would go in attempting an explanation. Well, let it pass.

During the night *Happy Adventure*'s Baddeck mud pack had begun to wear perilously thin. So we put in to Borden, Prince Edward Island, and there we found a bank of lovely, sticky, red, island clay upon which the schooner was persuaded to perch her backside for a few hours. When we departed from Borden she was tight again, but as she chuffed slowly westward she left behind her a spoor that spread a sanguinary hue upon the waters. She looked as if she were slowly bleeding to death.

We continued through the strait and next day put in to the Acadian port of Richibucto, New Brunswick, to fill our fuel tanks. From Jack's point of view this was a bad choice. He is so fantastically allergic to all crustacea, and to lobsters in particular, that close contact with them literally makes him lose his breath, and he breaks out in flaming and intolerably itchy welts all over his body. Richibucto is one of the world's great lobster ports, and the lobster season was in full flower.

As we lay at the dock the lobster boats began streaming home to harbour. They had had a good day's fishing. Since we were strangers, and therefore to be treated with traditional Acadian-French hospitality, many of the fishermen tossed gift lobsters in our cockpit as they passed by.

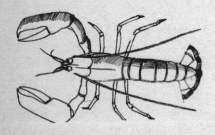 

As lobsters flew about us Jack began to wheeze, and to run up and down the decks like a dog kept too long away from a fire hydrant. When the barrage failed to diminish he began to scratch himself and his face began to crimson. With a low moan he leapt for the dock, climbed up on it, and stood there a moment peering about him as one pursued by unseen devils. There was no refuge for him there. The dock was jammed with lobster trucks, lobster crates, and lobsters in their thousands.

He fled down the dock, trotting urgently past the puzzled fishermen until he reached the beach – but even there he was not safe. He was followed by a small boy offering him a bucket of lobster claws.

Finally he sought sanctuary in a grassy swale a quarter of a mile up the shore, and there he sat, swatting moodily at mosquitoes, until I finished my leisurely chores, stowed our lobsters in a tin toolbox in the engine room, and signalled to him that all was clear.

I hope the good fishermen of Richibucto will forgive me, but once we were well at sea again I returned the lobsters to their native element. I had to do it. There was no way we were going to get on with our voyage as long as my mate had to spend all his time, and occupy both his hands, trying to alleviate a remorseless itch.

We sailed all that night, passed by Escuminac, and began the long haul across the broad and treacherous mouth of Chaleur Bay. Jack celebrated our departure from sight of land by indulging in a fit of absent-mindedness.

I had ordered him to stream the log; the brass cylinder on the end of a long log-line which recorded the distance run. He streamed it all right, but forgot to make the end of the line fast to the boat. I shall long cherish the memory of his face as he stood on the afterdeck, peering with a puzzled expression at his empty hands through which the last few inches of line had just run free. Despite the loss of the log, a cherished antique, I could not forbear laughing – and that was foolish of me. When, an hour later, we began to run into gale conditions and I decided to put back to Miscou for the night, Jack turned on me.

"Put back? God almighty, that's all you *ever* do! If you had the guts of a canary you'd hold your course. Afraid to die, are you? Bloody coward!"

I was very much afraid to die, but I was also afraid of having to live with Jack in future years unless I took his dare.

The crossing of Chaleur Bay was a wicked experience. We spent the night bucketing through some of the worst weather I have ever seen. Even the excellent Prince Edward Island clay could not keep its hold in the fearful seaway that was tossing us about like an ice-cube in a cocktail shaker. The clay washed out of *Happy Adventure*'s seams, and we were soon in a sinking condition and desperately looking for a landfall.

We eventually found one at Grande Rivière, a hamlet on the north shore of the bay, into which we pumped our way just before noon.

Grande Rivière was the first shore village we encountered that was not kind to men in little boats. It had no mud bank worthy of the name. The nearest approximation we could find was a peaty cutbank marking the shore side of somebody's cabbage garden. We backed *Happy Adventure* against this bank, and her counter hung right over the first row of cabbages. We were doing the cabbages no harm, but the owner of the garden, a sour old crone with a piercing voice, thought otherwise. She stood on the shore and harangued us until Jack lost patience. Assuming his most menacing scowl he glared down at her and in a thickly accented voice informed her that we were two officers of the Soviet Navy, sailing our small boat from Leningrad to Expo 67.

"Een Rahssia, old vimmen who makes too much noise we poot to slee-eep!" he told her, and made as if to jump ashore.

She fled in haste, and we were still chuckling about the incident half an hour later when we noticed two car-loads of Quebec Provincial Police pull up at the side of the highway a quarter of a mile from us, and pile out to form a squad armed with riot guns.

"You and your jokes!" I said bitterly as I dived for the engine. Jack said nothing. He was too busy straining to help the diesel get us off the shore into deep water.

Still leaking, *Happy Adventure* fled out into Chaleur Bay seeking a more hospitable haven. It was a bright and sunny

248

day. It soon became so hot that we were moved to strip off all our clothes as we pumped our way around Cap d'Espoir, and opened a stunning view of Bonaventure Island, Percé Rock, and the towering Gaspé cliffs beyond. For almost the first time on the voyage up through the gulf we had a favouring wind and as we closed with Percé Rock, our tanned sails set and drawing, we must have added considerably to the picturesqueness of the scene. At any rate we attracted the attention of a big sightseeing boat loaded with tourists.

The captain of the boat changed course to bring his herd of gawkers close alongside *Happy Adventure*, and as a score of cameras began to click, Jack, who is a gentleman first and foremost, uncoiled himself from his position in the cockpit, stood up to his full height, and bowed formally toward the array of glittering lenses.

Alas, this courteous gesture was not appreciated. The captain of the cruise boat thrust an enraged face out of his steering cabin and began cursing at us in piquant French. Several male passengers waved their fists at us. Others shook their cameras. One particularly solidly built matron stood up, at great risk to herself, and bellowed something about "filthy nudists." The tour boat put on speed and tore away in high dudgeon leaving us bewildered and not a little hurt.

"Ah, well," said Jack resignedly as he settled his sun-burned carcass back in the cockpit. "That's what you get for trying to be nice to people. Let it be a lesson to you, Mowat."

Once beyond Cap Gaspé, and properly into the estuary of the mighty St. Lawrence River, our progress slowed from a healthy snail's pace, to that of a badly crippled one. This was not entirely *Happy Adventure*'s fault, although our anxious search for suitable mud banks, in almost every little port we passed, inevitably resulted in some delay.

The major difficulty was that we were now "going up-hill." When the tide flowed against us, as it did for twelve hours out of every twenty-four, it combined with the current of the great river to set us back toward the gulf at from three to five knots. Since our maximum speed was not much *better* than five knots, there were times when we spent hours virtually sitting in the same place. This enabled us to have a leisurely look at the magnificent scenery, but it had a bad effect upon Jack's temper. When he originally assessed the length of time it would take us to reach Montreal he had probably been subconsciously thinking in terms of a motor torpedo boat capable of making forty knots. At any rate he had failed to allow for head winds, head tide, head seas and head currents.

One day we spent an entire morning staring at the unchanging shape of Fame Point looming a few miles ahead of us, and by noon Jack was fuming.

"Christ Almighty," he burst out. "We could swim to Montreal faster than this!"

He was overstating the case a little, but was not far enough off the mark that I cared to argue with him. I kept my peace because, although he was not yet aware of it, we *were* changing our position in regard to Fame Point. We were getting farther and farther away from it!

It was just plain bad luck that at this juncture we should be overtaken by a Montreal-bound freighter going west at about fifteen knots. It was not the freighter that set the seal on Jack's unhappiness – it was the spectacle of a handsome sailing yacht nestled contentedly on the freighter's deck: and the sight of three people whom we could only assume must be the crew of the yacht, taking their ease in deck chairs beside their pretty boat.

That night, when we parked *Happy Adventure* on a mud bank in the tiny port of L'Anse-à-Valleau, somewhat east of Fame Point, we had *lost* five miles of our precious westering.

We also lost Jack McClelland. For the second time in his experience with our little vessel, he was forced to leave her somewhat short of her destination. About nine hundred miles short of it.

Jack felt badly about abandoning me on this remote coast but, as he had done before, he swore he would find me a new mate. I did not believe him, since neither of us knew a soul within hundreds of miles of L'Anse-à-Valleau. Jack departed in a hired car for Gaspé, forty miles away, leaving me despondent and alone and faced with the awful prospect of having to proceed single-handed – if I was to proceed at all.

Three hours later I was roused from my gloomy ruminations below decks by a hail from the wharf.

"Is that the boat called the *Unhappy Misadventure?*"

Now I occasionally allow myself to say uncomplimentary things about my vessel, but no one else is going to do it with impunity. Stung to the quick I leapt up the companionway.

"Who the hell wants to know?" I yelled angrily.

Far above me (it was low tide, and the schooner's deck was twenty feet below the level of the wharf) a tousled head of hair appeared against the sky. Below it was a young, sunburned face whose innocent blue eyes looked down at me with some timidity.

"Sorry, sir, but Mr. Macklunon said I was to look for a boat of that name. I'm supposed to be her mate."

I invited the owner of the face aboard and all six-foot-lanky-six of him crawled awkwardly down the iron ladder. He introduced himself as Glen Wilson, age twenty-one, formerly a Pfc in the u.s. armed forces, now a free wanderer upon the face of the globe. Having left the u.s. Army rather suddenly after a disagreement about the validity of the Vietnam war, Glen had smartly betaken himself across the border into British Columbia, and was hitch-hiking his way eastward to Newfoundland. He had been standing on a bridge at Gaspé when a car pulled up alongside him and, as he described it:

"A flashy looking guy with blond hair got out, looked me over, and asked me had I ever sailed a boat. I told him, no, I'd never even been *in* a boat. He asked would I like to try it once, and heck, I thought, why not? Next thing I knew I was in the car and he was telling the French driver something. Then he shook my hand, told me I was going to go on the schooner, *Unhappy Misadventure*, bound for Montreal, and here I am. I hope you don't mind too much."

I was amused at first, then thoughtful. It seemed unlikely that this young foot-slogger would be of much assistance to me, but at least he would be company. I misjudged him. Glen was a natural-born sailor who was about to find his proper *métier* for the first time.

L'Anse-à-Valleau gave me more than a new mate – it gave me good advice. That evening a portly, dignified, French gentleman came to the wharf, and introduced himself as the retired captain of one of the unique St. Lawrence river vessels called *goélettes*. I told him something of my frustrations in trying to climb the hill, and he explained how it should be done.

We should, he told us, sail mainly at night when the prevailing westerly wind goes down; as far as possible we should make our runs with the rising tide; and we should stay within a mile of the shore in order to catch a series of reverse currents which set *up*stream instead of down.

That very night we put this new formula to the test, and it worked splendidly. By daybreak we were sixty miles west of Fame Point. This so heartened me that we kept going all that day and all of the next night, and might have kept going indefinitely had we not been forced to seek out another mud bank.

However we were now on a coast where mud banks simply did not exist. After trying two or three little harbours we had to settle for a sawdust pile; the spillage from a lumber mill that had been dumped into a shallow basin forming an artificial bar. Although the sawdust treatment worked quite well, it did not measure up to Prince Edward Island clay. As a connoisseur of mud banks I can assert that the red clay of the island cannot be surpassed for certain nautical purposes.

Ever since leaving the Bras d'Or lakes, *Happy Adventure* had behaved moderately well, except of course for her leakage, which was chronic. She seemed to be not just resigned to the voyage, but actually enjoying it. However that mood did not last long after we began running into the ship traffic in the mouth of the river.

Apart from a few freighters we had met in the gulf, she had never really seen big ships before. When, one night, we encountered three liners, an aircraft carrier, a fifty-thousand-ton ore carrier, and scores of other vessels, all of which ignored us completely, and sent us scuttling like demented water spiders to avoid being run down, *Happy Adventure* balked.

She did so in her usual, inimitable style. We were under power about ten miles from Rimouski when an ear-splitting scream burst from the engine room. A moment later the engine stalled.

It did not take long to find the trouble. The reduction gearbox was so hot it glowed. When it cooled I found that every bearing and gear in it had melted or exploded. The high temperature lubricant in the box had mysteriously vanished. This seemed impossible, because I had checked the level and filled the box only the previous day. It was not, of course, impossible. At the bottom of the box was a drain plug whose existence I had never even suspected. *Happy Adventure* knew about it. I found it some days later, lying in the bilge, several feet distant from the box.

We sailed back to Rimouski, and there we stayed for ten interminable days while we waited for spare parts that apparently had to come from Outer Monogolia via camel post.

However the long wait at Rimouski was not a total loss. Moored near us was a weather-beaten and sadly neglected little schooner from somewhere in Nova Scotia. One day, when an onshore blow made our moorings uncomfortable, we moved over and lay alongside this schooner. Her story was an unhappy one – but it had a useful moral. She had been bought several years earlier by a young couple from Toronto who had then tried to sail her up the river. After wrestling with her for a month or more, her owners gave up, tied her up at Rimouski, and went away, never to return.

It was perhaps underhanded of me, but I arranged with the man who told me the story to come aboard *Happy Adventure* one night, and tell it again. When he was through I asked him what would happen to the forlorn little vessel.

"The government, they take her for wharfage fees," he said, and, brutally, "they sell her cheap to some fellow in the town. This winter he will haul her out and cut her up for firewood. Good riddance, too."

That night *Happy Adventure* did not leak a drop. When we departed for Quebec on September first, she behaved so well that we ran on by day and by night.

Glen had made such good progress as a sailor that I was able to entrust him with short tricks at the tiller while I napped below decks. We passed Murray Bay on a moonless, cloudy night that was as dark as pitch. At about one in the morning I was unable to keep awake any longer, so I gave Glen a course on the distant lighthouse at Goose Cape, telling him to steer for it until it was getting close, then to call me back on deck.

He did not call me, and at half past three I awoke feeling

vaguely conscious of something being not quite right. Sleepily I went on deck and looked about me. Far ahead – as far away as it had been when I went to my bunk – I saw a light.

"What the hell? . . ." I said to Glen who was sitting stolidly at the tiller. "We should have been abeam of Goose Cape light long ago. What the devil's happening? . . ."

"Couldn't say, Captain." He always called me Captain, a hangover from his army days perhaps. "It got closer for a while, but it sure don't get no closer now."

I looked at the compass, and the awful truth dawned on me. Somehow Glen had switched his attention from the light on Goose Cape to the bright masthead light of a big ship heading east down the southern channel. *Happy Adventure* was making about seven knots over the bottom, on a falling tide, and heading resolutely for salt water and for home. This time, however, nobody could lay the blame on her.

We came about and resumed our uphill course and, despite heavy traffic and a spell of abominable weather, we reached the Citadel City at dusk on September fourth. Montreal and Expo 67 now seemed just around the corner.

At Quebec *Happy Adventure* changed crews for the last time. If she had done nothing else during her chequered career, she could at least now lay claim to having been instrumental in leading one human being to a new way of life. Glen Wilson left us to sign on as ordinary seaman on a Norwegian freighter outbound for Pernambuco. The sea had claimed him.

Claire and Albert rejoined the ship and I was as glad to see them as they were to get aboard again. That evening we departed for Montreal.

The journey up river was anti-climactic. Still shivering at the fate that had befallen her Nova Scotian sister at Rimouski, *Happy Adventure* behaved like the angel she was not. The weather was inland summer weather: hot, muggy, almost windless. The river itself posed no problems because, while in Quebec, I had met the skipper of a *goélette*, and he had taught me the tricks involved in climbing the remaining slopes. We did as the *goélettes* did, riding the rising tide against the current, and anchoring in some snug cove when tide and current both flowed against us.

Our only immediate difficulty was with the river traffic. As the ship channels grew narrower, big ships grew more numerous. At one exceedingly narrow bend, just past the head of Lac St. Pierre, we found ourselves facing a twenty-thousand-ton downbound tanker – while being overtaken by an equally gigantic upbound grain carrier. Although neither of these behemoths bore us any ill will, it was impossible for them to alter course and so make room for us. We had to seek our own salvation. We sought it by scuttling right out of the channel into the shoal water, where the wake of the tanker struck us like a tidal wave and washed us almost high and dry on a spoil bank. Moments later the wake from the grain carrier, rebounding from the shore, washed us off and back into the channel again. Albert thought this was great fun. Claire and I wished fervently that we were back in the wide, grey, empty wastes of the North Atlantic.

From Trois Rivières, where we lost the last tidal influence, we entered still another world – a truly horrid one. This was the world of motor pleasure craft. Overpowered, overbearing, all over the channel, they made life hell for slow, deep-draft vessels like ours. Storming along at twenty knots, pushing half the river ahead of them and sucking the other half behind, they made more noise and disturbance than the big freighters; and most of their owners were not only devoid of elementary courtesy, but seemed to know nothing of the rules of the road, and to care less.

A torrent of these raucous, ostentatious toys made our final day on the river an ordeal. It was fearfully hot and we were near exhaustion, having run almost continuously from Trois Rivières. As the hours wore on and more and more power boats sent us pitching wildly in their wake we grew increasingly distraught. By the time we raised the unlovely skyline of oil refineries at the eastern edge of Montreal, and entered the stinking yellow pall of smoke they laid across the river, we were near the end of our tether.

Hot, sticky, dirty, and excessively tired, I began to wonder why we had gone to all this trouble to drag our little vessel from a world of cool and quiet peace to this brimstone cauldron. I was still wondering as we came abreast of the heart of Montreal and began trying to locate the fabulous goal at the end of this shoddy rainbow.

The harbour was as busy as a throughway. Ferries nipped across our bows and stern. Big ships hooted and boomed at us on all sides. Claire, at the tiller, was chivvied by a tug and its tow until she nearly burst into tears. I could see the towers, minarets and domes of Expo, but I could *not* see how I was going to reach them. At this juncture yet another motor boat bore down on us like a hyena on a hapless groundhog.

Only – this was no ordinary power boat. As she came foaming toward us her blue hull began to look familiar.

Painted huge on her bow was the inscription *MP 43* and suddenly I recognized her as the *Blue Heron*, sister ship to the *Blue Iris*.

"Oh my God!" I cried despairingly to Claire. "The blue doom has us!"

"The long claw of the Sea Puss gets us all, in the end," Claire replied unhelpfully. "Well, Skipper, let's see you talk your way out of this one."

The point was that we were flagrantly illegal. Not only did we fail to have our vessel's name on her bows, according to marine regulations, but we did not have our official number painted on them either, as is sternly required by the Canada Shipping Act. To make matters worse, we were not flying the prescribed Canadian ensign at our mainmast. We were flying the flag of the Basque provinces with, underneath it, as a courtesy to Quebec, the fleur-de-lis. I could only hope that *MP 43* did not know who we really were and that we might bluff our way to freedom.

Blue Heron throttled back abeam of us. A smartly uniformed Mountie with a loud-hailer stepped out on the bridge.

"Ahoy, the *Happy Adventure!* Follow me, please!"

And with that, the police vessel swung around our stern and took station dead ahead.

For one moment I was tempted to dive below, open the seacocks, and scuttle my ill-fated schooner; but the spirit had gone out of me. I was beaten, and I knew it.

Blue Heron led us up the harbour at a funereal pace until we neared a mighty breakwater in front of the islands upon which Expo towered. Four fast speedboats now appeared and raced toward us. The drivers had walkie-talkies, and were dressed in some sort of esoteric uniform I did not recognize.

Blue Heron now veered off, put on speed, and raced away while the four whining speedboats formed up, two ahead and two astern, shepherding *Happy Adventure* inexorably toward a gap in the seawall.

As we entered the narrow gap I was appalled to see puffs of blue smoke rise suddenly from the pierheads at either side.

We were deafened by a series of terrible concussions.

"Duck! For the love of God!" I screamed at Claire and Albert. "Now they're *shooting* at us!"

However Claire, brave woman that she is, did not flinch. Standing proudly at the bow she looked straight ahead, daring the Fates to do their worst. Albert stood beside her, solid and indomitable. They were a sight to make a man's heart catch with pride.

As the echoes of the fusillade died away, Claire spoke.

"Ooooooh, Farley," she cried ecstatically. "They're giving us a *reception* . . . isn't that *nice!*"

The words were barely uttered when we were deafened again, this time by such a cacophony of blasts, toots, whistles, hoots and screeches that I let go of the tiller and clapped my hands to my ears.

We had passed through the gap and directly ahead of us was a huge artificial basin containing what must have been one of the most glittering arrays of expensive yachts ever gathered together in one place. All of them were sounding their noisemakers. People stood on their decks, waving glasses and bottles and flags. The din was indescribable. I glanced over my shoulder expecting to see a Royal Yacht entering in our wake – but there was nothing to be seen. Slowly it was borne in upon me that, inconceivable as it seemed, all this hulla-baloo was being raised for us.

The speedboats guided us to the number one berth, directly in front of the main buildings of this exotic marina, and there we were moored by a quartet of eager young men between two floating palaces that, together, must have been worth the equivalent of a shah's ransom. A bosun piped us ashore to where a posse of officials waited. One of them made a little speech welcoming us to Montreal and to Expo 67, then a familiar face moved forward from the crowd. It belonged to a senior executive of Expo, and a friend from long ago.

I grabbed him by the arm.

"What in hell is this all about? I've never been so bloody scared in all my life!"

Grinning, he explained. In our remote fastness of Burgeo it had not occurred to us that the outer world would ever hear, or could possibly have cared, about our voyage. We had been wrong. Expo knew; Expo cared. From the time we passed the pilot station at Escuminac Point in the mouth of the river, Expo had been getting reports of our erratic progress. We had been under surveillance all that time.

"Mind you," my friend told us, "nobody ever expected you'd actually *make* it. The betting odds were twenty-five to one against. I lost a bit myself. I thought you'd sink for good long before you reached Quebec. The boat that wouldn't float! What'd you do? Fill her up with ping-pong balls?"

"Quiet!" I muttered urgently. "Don't *say* things like that. Not when she can hear you, anyway."

But I am afraid she must have heard.

That night we celebrated the end of fourteen hundred miles of struggle, of wrestling with adversity in all its manifold forms – in proper style.

It was late the next morning before we awoke. The sun was streaming into the cabin through the big forward port. I lay for a while and thought about the voyage. Then I turned my head toward Claire's bunk.

"Well, dear, it's all over now. Want some coffee? I'll put the kettle on."

I swung my legs out of my bunk . . . and stepped into twelve inches of cold water.

She had done it again.

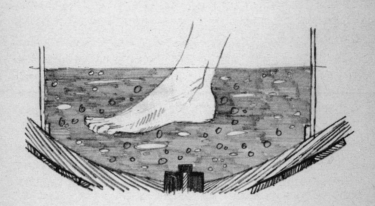

21· *Envoi*

For the next five days Expo repented of its folly in welcoming the boat that wouldn't float. *Happy Adventure* had opened up so badly that we could only keep her head above water by continuous pumping with several electric pumps, and the somewhat malodorous jets that these flung against the millionaire yachts to either side of us were not appreciated. Expo officials kept moving us farther and farther into the hinterland of the Marina. We never saw our executive friend again, and he probably wished he had *never* seen us. All our efforts to staunch the leaks failed, and finally, in absolute desperation, we sailed our sinking vessel out of there, heading west in hopes of finding either a mud bank or a shipyard before it was too late.

We needed neither. Two hours after she left Expo, *Happy Adventure* stopped leaking, as suddenly and as inexplicably as she had begun.

A week later she, and we, arrived at the little Lake Ontario town of Port Hope, where Claire and I had bought a house. There were no facilities there to haul the vessel, so she had to stay in the water that winter. She did not like it.

In January, when she was surrounded by ice not quite strong enough to bear a man's weight, she opened up again. We saved her – just – but I had two memorable and unintentional swims amongst the ice-floes, while trying to reach her from the shore.

This being almost the last straw, I had her hauled that spring at Deseronto, on the Bay of Quinte, and she spent most of 1968 ashore, while experts came and looked at her, and probed, and fiddled, and admitted themselves baffled. Once in a while we would launch her on trial. She would leak like a sieve, so we would haul her up again. By the end of the summer I was ready to abandon hope. I told Don Dawson, the shipyard owner, to tear the engine out of her, strip her of anything useful, and let her die.

Don is a strange sort of a man. He cannot easily endure defeat. Without consulting me, he made one last attempt to discover *Happy Adventure*'s fatal flaw. One October day he phoned me.

"Farley? Listen now. I launched your boat last week. She's been sitting in the water ever since, and *she hasn't leaked a drop*. I think I've found the trouble."

Of course I did not believe him, but being an eternal optimist I was persuaded to rescind her death sentence.

A few days before she was due to be launched in the spring of 1969 I visited her. As always, she looked a bit ungainly out of water, and she looked totally alien amongst the rows of slick motor-cruisers and fibreglass yachts. She was a sad, forlorn little ship; and I was suddenly stricken with guilt.

I thought to myself that she had been good to me in her way, and loyal too. And I thought what a dirty trick it was to bring her into exile in this land of fresh (polluted) water, toy boats and play boats, and there to let her rot her heart away.

On a sudden impulse I said, "Never mind, old girl. I'll tell you what. Come summer, if you stay afloat and mind your P's and Q's, I'll take you back where you belong. What do you say to that?"

She said nothing then, but as I write these words she has been afloat for a month, is tight as a drum, and is in better health than I have ever known her to enjoy. That is her answer. So one of these days Claire and I and Albert and

Happy Adventure will turn eastward, down the long, long river, to the salt and living sea; to the silence and the fog; to the world in which my little ship was born. *Happy Adventure* will be going home.

About the Author

Farley Mowat was born in Belleville, Ontario, in 1921, and grew up in Belleville, Trenton, Windsor, Saskatoon, Toronto and Richmond Hill, following his librarian father Angus Mowat's peregrinations around the country. He served in World War II from 1940 until 1945, entering the army as a private and emerging with the rank of captain. He began writing for his living in 1949 after spending two years in the Arctic. Since 1949 he has lived in or visited almost every part of Canada and many other lands including the distant regions of Siberia. He remains an inveterate traveller with a passion for remote places and peoples. He has twenty-two books to his name, which have been published in translations in over twenty languages in more than forty countries. They include such internationally known works as *People of the Deer*, *The Dog Who Wouldn't Be*, *Never Cry Wolf*, *Westviking*, *Sibir* and *A Whale for the Killing*. His short stories and articles have appeared in the *Saturday Evening Post*, *Maclean's*, *Atlantic Monthly* and other magazines.